PARENT to
PARENT
Raising Children from Prison

By William J. Patterson

Freebird Publishing
North Dighton, MA

Freebird Publishers

Box 541, North Dighton, MA 02764
Info@FreebirdPublishers.com
www.FreebirdPublishers.com

ISBN-13: 978-1-952159-10-7

Printed in the United States of America

This book is dedicated to my mother Teresa and my late father Dennis. Thank you for loving me the best way you knew how.

This book is also dedicated to all parents inside and out, along with their children. May your love for each other bridge every separation.

Acknowledgments

I want to take this moment to share my sincere gratitude to all of you who helped make this book possible. Your unrelenting encouragement, love, and support are a blessing in my life.

First off, I want to thank God. Thank you for all that has been, all that is, and all that will be. Thank you for your unconditional love and helping me to discover it in myself. Please continue to guide me and inspire me in all that I do.

I am indebted to my great friend, mentor, and confidant Thomas J., not only for his continued support but his faith in my abilities to see this project through. He spent countless hours with me to make edits and put together the many aspects of this book. His unwavering assistance helped me make this book become a reality. What's more, he has devoted many hours of his time actively listening to my life's stories and guiding me to become more aware and awake.

Thank you to my friends who have continued to support me throughout the years: Tom, Mitch, Greg, Larry, Pat, Jennifer, and others. May our friendships continue to grow for many years to come.

Thank you to my many 12-step "Celebrate Recovery" brothers for allowing me to share my life with you and for sharing yours with me. And I give a special thanks to my sponsor Darrin G. During those times of sharing, I learned that I was not alone in my struggles, and, although flawed, I am loved by many.

To my family: Kathy, Kay, Susan, Mary, Geraldine, and others, I want to thank you for your continued love and support throughout my life and this tumultuous period of my incarceration. Your letters and support have meant everything. Please know that sharing my life, throughout this book, is in no way meant to embarrass or diminish our family or its history. It's my prayer that, by sharing my past, I can inspire others to make needed changes that will help them transform their lives and receive the many blessings and gifts of wisdom that my family has provided me.

To my little brother Greg: I am sincerely sorry for the many times you needed me over the years, and I failed you. If I could go back and do it differently, I certainly would. You have continued to be a tremendous help to me as I prepare to make the transition home and face the world with all its challenges. Thank you for your love and support. I look forward to sharing our lives in the years ahead.

To my parents Dennis and Teresa: thank you for giving me life; thank you for loving me the best and only way you knew how, for accepting me just the way I am, flaws and all. Without both of you, I would not be here today, nor would this book have been possible. Sharing our life's experiences, no matter what they entailed, helped spark a change in me and hopefully will help spark changes in others as they try to discover themselves on this path, we call life. I will always love you mom and dad; thank you with all my heart.

An enormous thank you goes out to the two most amazing and wonderful human beings that I know – my two sons. Each of you has been a rock to hold onto during this storm. You have suffered great losses and pain as a result of my past actions. You have endured my physical absence during your birthdays, holidays, and other special occasions. Although not always successful, I tried to be the best father I could from prison, and yet through it all, you continue to love and believe in me. You guys are my greatest joy. There are no words that can encompass my unconditional love for each of you. I look forward to each and every remaining moment we have left to share together in this life and beyond.

I want to thank Diane at Freebird Publishers yet again for allowing my voice to be heard in my work. Thank you for believing in me and helping make this book a reality. Together we are changing lives and making a difference. Thank you!

I have tried to recall the events in this book to the best of my ability. If any errors have been made in structure, style, or content the responsibility rests entirely on my shoulders.

Sincerely,

William J. Patterson

William J. Patterson

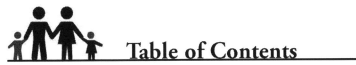

Table of Contents

Introduction

The essence of being parents is learning to be true to ourselves and owning our beauty as well as our scars, to focus on not what once was but rather what is, and to live with love, tolerance, and compassion. May we be aware of our limitations, not defined by them.

As I write this book, I am coming to the end of my 9-year federal prison sentence. I never dreamed on that horrific first day of this ordeal that I would one day be writing about it, much less sharing some of my life's most intimate feelings with the world. The abrupt separation from my two children – then both under the age of ten – was devastating to me since I was very close to them and played a major role in their lives. The separation felt as if someone had taken away a part of me. There was a void I could not fill. The pain was immense, and the agony consumed me. In addition, I had the pain of so many regrets from my past decisions to deal with. I began to realize the impact of my previous choices and the affect they had on my family and me.

My children are now teenagers. It's been very challenging being away from them all these years and having limited visits. Looking back, I realize how often I've drawn strength from-their mere existence. Trying to be an ideal father from behind these fences has not been without failures. There's no such thing as a perfect father, but there are real ones. I realized that if the world were perfect it would be meaningless and growing would not be necessary. We are put here to love and learn. Isn't that what wisdom is all about?

Now that I am nearing the end of my sentence, I have time to look back and reflect. I see just how much I've grown as both a human being and as a father. It hasn't been without obstacles and pain. But growth is painful, I've come to learn. I have spent thousands of hours taking every available class and have read many books in the effort to learn things new and beneficial to my life. Many of these classes and books involved parenting and self-improvement. At times, it felt as though I was trying to swim in what seemed like an immense ocean with intense waves trying to pull me under. Not all of my efforts at fathering from prison were successful or even productive for that matter. Yet if by sharing both the positive and negative experiences of my life as a father with others can help just one parent succeed, it will all be worth it.

Sharing my past ignorance by exposing my failures feels very vulnerable to me. Frankly, I don't like it. Nevertheless, I've learned that real life requires, although frightening at times, my honesty. More importantly, life demands I tell the truth if I want to continue to grow as a person and be a good father.

It's my belief that in order to live a fulfilled life, we have to begin thinking now about the end, so we can make each moment count. With life comes death, none of us knows how long we have left on this earth. Each letter, phone call, visit or breath could be our last. Each day, each moment is a gift. Tomorrow may never come. The present moment is the only moment we have. I say all of that to say this: If you do not remember anything else in this book, please remember that it's never too late to say "I love you" to your children or anyone else you love for that matter. Never! Never! Never!

Who to Blame

"We have a hunger of the mind which asks for knowledge of all around us, and the more we gain, the more is our desire; the more we see, the more we are capable of seeing."

– Maria Mitchell (1818-1889)

On a crisp fall afternoon in 2012, my world as I knew it came grinding to a halt after my arrest. I have replayed the events in my mind a thousand times over. In shock and absolute disbelief, I was devastated by what was actually happening to me. I recall the shame and humiliation like it was yesterday. The horrific memories are burned into my mind. It took a few weeks for the reality to set in and my anger to surface.

In the beginning, I was most angry at the person who called the police but also very angry at God. How could God allow something so devastating to happen to me? I admit that my daily prayer for years had been to help me be a better man and person. But "hell no God," this is not what I was praying for by any stretch of the imagination.

I'm not afraid to say that I cursed God with all my might. Eventually, as the months slowly passed and I read more and more scripture, I realized that God, or my idea of God at the time, really had nothing to do with this. I imagined Him as simply sitting there looking down at me thinking, "How am I to blame for this, I didn't do it?" It was during this revelation that I realized I was looking for someone else to blame besides myself. I mean after all; this couldn't be my fault.

At that time, I began to shift blame to my parents, especially my dad. I was thinking that if they had done a better job at parenting none of this would have happened. Regardless of these emotions, my inner conflicts and turmoil, my mother was at my side throughout all my court proceedings but not my father.

My dad and I had an estranged relationship. We had been distant as far back as I can remember. Our relationship was more like two men who were acquainted rather than our sharing a father/son bond, or at least that was my perception at the time. I had always felt at odds with him and out-of-touch. Even when I took my own children to visit and spend time with him, I never could feel a sense of closeness or love.

Two of the greatest emotions I experienced with my dad were rejection and feeling under-valued. I carried a large amount of anger and resentment towards my dad. Years later during my incarceration, intense self-help studies and therapy, I came to realize the much resentment I held towards my dad was also held towards my mother and brother. This all stemmed from my developmental years and family experiences. I also discovered during this self-reflection and study that underneath all that anger and resentment were buckets of hurt and fear.

Right at the one-year mark and prior to my transfer to moving a longer distance from my family, my dad was able to visit me for an hour. Even though I was behind a glass, I was able to see his smile. He seemed in good spirits considering the circumstances. At times, I wonder about the immense pain and disappointment he must have felt but kept hidden from me. That was the last time I ever got to see him alive. As the years passed his health continued to deteriorate and eventually, he died on November 19, 2015. I will never forget the officer waking me around 11:00 p.m. in order to inform me of this great loss.

During the years between my arrest and my father's death, I had sent him numerous letters. I remember saying how sorry I was and declaring that none of this was his fault. I tried to recall all the memorable and enjoyable moments that he and I shared. As a last-ditch effort to connect with him, I wrote one time explaining that if he couldn't think of anything to write, a simple "I love and miss you" would work. He never responded to my request. No words in writing from him were ever received. I took this lack of response as one more rejection of me. It hurt deeply, especially when I needed him more than ever in my life. Occasionally when talking to my mom, I had brief moments to chat with my dad over the phone. Eventually when given the opportunities, I simply declined to speak with him. I could not bear any further rejection from him. I felt as though I could no longer beg or force him to express his love for me the way I wanted to be loved. The wound I carry still resides within me today, but much healing has taken place. I like to say that I am a work in progress.

My current relationship with my mother and brother is probably on the best terms they have ever been – but not without literally hundreds of hours of my dedicated and persistent self-examination, 12-step group meetings, psychology classes, counseling, spiritual growth and my relationship with God.

Sharing so much personal and intimate information about family is not easy. However, it's real life and involves real people. It is my intention that readers can relate my experiences to some of their own and use my story as an inspiration not to give up but rather to repair any damaged relationships, especially with their children. I realized that in order to be the best dad possible I needed to look deep within myself and examine all the areas that needed improvement. I also had to look closely at my own family dynamics, and how it played a role in my behavior, beliefs and actions.

I mentioned previously about my mom's continued support throughout my court proceedings so rather than blame her, I want to praise her. I want to take a moment here to give her the credit she deserves. Let the truth be told: She has never left my side. Any attributes she may have lacked as a mother during my childhood, she has more than made up for during my years of incarceration. She continues to go above and beyond what I deserve. Every visit that has ever occurred with my children was made possible because of my mother's sacrifices. Mom's willingness and efforts have never faltered. At times, she drove four hours each way just for a 30-minute visit. Thank you, Mom, I owe you more than I could ever repay. Good mother's make good fathers possible.

I mentioned my children in the introduction. I must admit that I have been very fortunate in many ways as an incarcerated father. I want to take a moment to express my sincere gratitude to my children's mother. I will be indebted to her for the remainder of my life: first, for blessing me with two wonderful souls and second for her continued cooperation in allowing me to remain an active father in their lives throughout my incarceration.

To say that my arrest was a disappointment to her is an understatement; however, she has never prevented a visit or interrupted any of my letters or phone calls to our children. She is happily married, and I am also grateful to her husband as a stepfather, who has done his best at protecting and guiding our children as if they were his own.

What has been your experience and circumstances when it comes to the children of incarcerated parents? I have met my share of fathers who have lost all contact with their children as a result of their incarceration. Each time I hear this it pains my heart, and as a father I can relate to the agony they are experiencing.

For those of you who may be in this category, I encourage you not to give up hope, to live each day as if your child is still in your life, and to take responsibility for your actions, including any errors or oversights. I suggest you apologize to them and make amends where appropriate. Doing so is conducive to success and to a sense that you are in control of your life, not a victim of fate. Remember, everybody makes mistakes. Mistakes are our best teachers, so don't waste their lessons. Acknowledge them, learn from them, and become more competent because of them.

2

Grief and Loss

"There is no pain greater than this; not the cut of a jagged-edged dagger nor the fire of a dragon's breath. Nothing burns in your heart like the emptiness of losing something, someone, before you truly have learned its value."

— Robert Salvatore (1959-)

Being incarcerated comes with many challenges. Grief and loss are a big part of those. Besides your freedom a person's losses may include: the loss of material goods, relationships, jobs, control, identity, dreams, goals, and a loved one's death. The first need in coping with a loss is to realize and accept that it has occurred. Then you can take the necessary measures to cope with it. My losses include many of those listed above.

Although the process is a painful one, the second need of mourning a loss is to enter the pain of that loss. Through self-study and counseling, I've learned that grieving is a process that requires six needs of mourning. Furthermore, grief is the inner thoughts and feelings that occur after a loss. Mourning a loss is the expression of those thoughts and feelings in whatever way is appropriate to you.

I've found that the loss of control is one of the most difficult losses for me to integrate into my life. It still sneaks up on me, and I have to check myself on a moment-by-moment basis. I like to see it as one of my character defects. I use that language based on my self-discovery in 12-step meetings. I found 12-step study very beneficial in helping me make needed changes and cope with issues like self-control or lack thereof.

One way that I was able to take control of myself was accepting 100% responsibility for my actions and letting go of everything else. I continually remind myself that I have no control over anything that happens in the world except for what I do, what I say, what I think, and how I choose to respond to the events of this day. What's more, I've learned that the results of my efforts are not within my control; however, I can still put forth an effort. I can still make a difference regardless of the obstacles I face.

For those of you who may not have direct access to your children, don't let this discourage you from putting forth your best efforts to reach-out and connect. Have you ever considered writing a journal or a book for your child to present to them at a later date? What about writing letters to your child and forwarding them to a family or friend for safe keeping? Remember, your children will one day become an adult, and what you have written and shared over the years could be the steppingstone to true healing for your child.

For those of you with adult children, the effort is yours to make but the results will remain out of your hands. Use your imagination for different ways to connect and know that change is constant. It's ever evolving, and a person may not feel the same today as they did yesterday. Don't miss that opportunity.

The loss of my material goods cut like a double-edged sword. On one hand, the financial cost of my arrest was exponential. In the end, I lost all of my vehicles, personal belongings, savings, retirement funds, and even my home. Currently my release status is designated as homeless. On the other hand, after integrating the above losses through the mourning process, I chose not to allow my financial ruin to dictate my future. Even though the hurt of these losses cut deep, they provided a way for me to see more clearly the loss of more precious things, like my freedom and access to my family and friends. This allowed me to look deeper into the grief and losses in my life that remained unresolved.

The loss of my father through death remains a loss that I continue to work through. I realize that I have not fully grieved his passing and absence from my life. However, I have made some progress using self-help study guides, journaling, prayer, and sharing with others the feelings that I experience as it relates to him, which happens to meet the third need in the mourning process – expressing the thoughts and feelings of the loss.

Don't be surprised if you also feel these feelings after your loss: sadness, loneliness, guilt, blame, helplessness, fear, anger, relief, and shame. All of them need to be expressed appropriately; otherwise, they show up in self-destructive ways, I've learned. None of these feelings are wrong.

Feelings are not right or wrong, good or bad. Feelings just are. There is no need to twist yourself into knots trying to avoid any of these. In fact, expressing them shows that you are a human being capable of caring about another person. They can be painful, and it's natural to want to avoid them, but don't. Resist the temptation to hide them. Express them in a way that is natural and appropriate to you.

Prior to my incarceration, many of my unhealthy habits were used as a mechanism to avoid feeling these painful feelings. My self-destructive habits were detrimental to my livelihood, well-being, relationships, and health. They contributed to countless problems in my life and eventually cost me the ultimate price – my freedom.

The solution that I've discovered is to grieve and mourn in a healthy way. These feelings can be resolved and will pass. It is important to remember that they are only feelings, that they are not you but rather a small part of you that comes and goes. Events do not cause our emotions, we do. Ultimately, we decide how we feel, yet the expression of our feelings is a critical part of the mourning process when we've experienced a great loss and are in grief about it.

Remember that grief is the internal thoughts and feelings about the losses you've suffered, and mourning is the expression of those thoughts and feelings. The first three needs of mourning have been discussed – acknowledging the reality of the loss, entering the pain of the loss, and expressing your thoughts and feelings about the loss. However, the other three needs of mourning are just as important.

After your loss experience a major shift in your life takes place, an identity change occurs - the fourth need of mourning. You no longer are the person you were before the loss occurred and now you must adjust your self-understanding and place in the world, without the person or objects you've lost. As I have mentioned, the loss of my father has caused me to forge a new identity as a son without a father, and the loss of my freedom has brought about a whole new me. I can truly say that I am not the same man who entered this prison seven years ago. I can also declare that I am a more attuned, aware, and loving father to my children than I was before I lost my freedom.

Grief about a loss is devastating and can paralyze us, and it can even imprison us from others and ourselves. Don't I know this; but mourning can be our path to release and freedom.

One's need to ask and seek the answers to life's most difficult questions becomes the fifth need of the mourning process. Where do I come from? Who am I? What is my purpose in life? What happens after we die? How do I make things right? Before my series of losses, I didn't consider the above questions. It wasn't until I found myself facing the unknown without my family, friends, career, hopes, identity and death, did I begin to ask the above questions about my purpose, my truth, my goodness, and my existence.

After all that I had lost, I felt alone; devastated, ruined, worthless and so forth. I had no idea how and why I ended up in prison until I began to question, to seek, and to get support, which meets the sixth need of mourning – seek the support of others in the mourning process.

Because of my losses, I had to admit that I needed help and that I was vulnerable. Once that obstacle of pride dissolved my walls of fear and shame, I discovered the helping hands and hearts of family members, friends, chaplains, fellow inmates, and even strangers. The mourning process isn't easy, and it remains an ongoing challenge to integrate the many losses we suffer along our unique paths; but it sure is good to know that we are not alone, that you are not alone, even in the darkest moments of your life.

3

Facing Our Fears

"Fear is the path to the dark side. Fear leads to anger. Anger leads to hate. Hate leads to suffering."

– "Yoda," George Lucas (1944-)

Typically, all of us parents have fears about our children. We worry about doing the right thing or wrong thing. We worry about doing it the right way or wrong way. We also worry how our past actions may affect our children's future. We all want a bright and happy future for our children. As an incarcerated parent, the one fear that seems magnified more than all the rest is the fear of rejection.

Rejection is painful. I do not know of anything else that can ravage one's heart like rejection. No wound penetrates more than rejection from our own children. I think execution itself would be easier to endure than abandonment by my child. The feelings of devastation and sorrow when a child rejects us chips away at our self-worth and our confidence as parents. It challenges our sense of hope while the memory of our children's faces and voices linger in our minds like silent haunting messages saying that we are not wanted and unworthy of their love. During times like these, heartbroken and crushed, we must reach deep within ourselves to discover the truth of who we really are. We must look within ourselves, as well as to our higher power, and to family and friends to help sustain us through this process of self-discovery.

I have firsthand experience of rejection by one of my children. Prior to my incarceration, he and I were extremely close. We had a bond that I thought to be unbreakable. Our bond remained very tight over the years until he became a teenager. In his teenage years, he began to distance himself from me, eventually spelling it out with words. His words, although written in a respectful manner, cut my heart to its core. He informed me that my past actions were "horrible," that he would have to live with them for the rest of his life, and that he no longer wanted to ever come and visit me again. He went on to say that no kid wants to go inside a prison. I believe that comment stems from great fear and shame that he himself has experienced during the visitation process. Everyone handles and processes events differently. He wrote that he is not upset that I am gone but upset over me being an embarrassment to him. He wrote that he no longer wants me in his life and that he wants to be left alone. He also stated that he does not want me getting out of prison early because he does not wish to associate with me. He did acknowledge the fact that I will always be his dad and that I have tried to be a good dad from prison. However, he disagrees about forgiving a father and does not want to forgive me. He wishes to live a happy life and cannot do that with me in it. He said he was sorry that things had to be this way.

I did not include my son's comments and rejection in order to seek self-pity. I shared them because it's real and painful and because it provides a permanent example of the process we've previously discussed. He has experienced loneliness, sadness, loss, grief, abandonment, rejection, fear, and much more. What's more, it is indicative of just how deeply a parent's action can harm their children. His words were the most difficult that I have ever read, not only for hearing his pain, but for realizing that I was the cause of it. After receiving his response, I had to look deep within myself for how to proceed. I gave careful thought, prayed, and shared his response with my closest friends. Sometimes surrendering to the truth means giving up trying to understand and becoming comfortable with uncertainty, to go beyond the wants and fears in a relationship, and to remember that real love does not want, fear, or demand anything. True love is given freely. I will discuss the response to my son later in chapter 6.

Being forgotten by the children you love is another common fear, especially for those of us who are locked away hundreds of miles from them. These long separations and limited contact can wreak havoc on our relationships. When we think of our children forgetting us as their parents, our hearts break. Despite our fear of being forgotten, and even though we may be hurt and isolated, as parents, we must make the effort and take the initiative to reach out to our children in whatever way possible regardless of the obstacles. I have made it a point over the years, regardless of what type of response or lack of response I receive from my children, that I would continue to build a bridge to them through my efforts to communicate. For example, I would send letters to them and expect a response and when I didn't get a response or the response I wanted, I had to remind myself that they were either too busy having fun or not yet capable to respond in an appropriate or timely manner. I had to learn, once again, to love them as they are in the moment and to accept what is rather than how I want them to be. Once again, these occasions reminded me that being a parent is about taking care of my children's needs above and beyond my own, and when I put my children first, I never feel forgotten.

If we as parents are gone for an extended period of time, it is entirely possible for another person to be introduced into our children's lives. As a result, you may have experienced the fear of being replaced. This may be a boyfriend or stepparent. You may experience feelings of anger, rage, or loss. You may fear that your child will bond with this new person in your place. What we must remember is that we are powerless over this, and we can only hope that our children's caregiver chooses a responsible and caring person as a role model. No matter how great a person may be, they can never replace you. I've learned for instance, that I do not have to feel less than because of my children's stepfather, but rather, I can be grateful for his love and guidance to my children. He is fulfilling his role as a stepfather, and I still have mine to fill as their father.

Until we resolve the fear of being forgotten and replaced, we will continue to wrestle with an even more powerful fear: our fear of being powerless. The loss of our agency and autonomy is a horrible feeling. In other words, as incarcerated parents we want to help and contribute, but our inability to do so makes it extremely painful. It can cause a parent to doubt his/her self-worth. This has been a huge challenge for me during my incarceration. Prior to my arrest, I was a provider and protector to my children. Since incarceration, I have been unable to physically protect them or financially contribute to my children's development. I felt completely powerless. In response to my fear, I have empowered myself as you can see by continually searching for other ways or areas that can contribute to my children's growth and well-being (see chapter 9). Powerlessness is merely a temporary state and when faced head-on it provides you opportunities for self-improvement, self-knowledge, and self-empowerment.

In addition to the above fears, I fear I may have permanently harmed my children by my past actions and by being incarcerated. It appears to be a common occurrence for us incarcerated parents to feel great shame for our past decisions by thinking that by our past choices alone we have ruined our children's lives. We may even think that our children have no chance of success. Some may even go as far as thinking that the child would be better off without them and, as a result, cut off any communication or connection.

Because it has worked for me, I suggest instead of severing ties, breaking bonds, or turning away, use these fears to motivate you into being a better and stronger parent. You'll find that although children are affected by incarceration, they are strong and resilient in so many ways, stronger than anybody can know until they are seen and heard. Stop being your own greatest critic. Instead, become your greatest advocate. You might have made a bad choice in the past, but you are a good person who is worthy of love, and your love must begin with yourself. You have to love yourself to be able to fully love your children and others. And in turn, by loving others you will learn to better love yourself.

I don't know about you, but my greatest fear would be to lose all contact with my children. Although my visits with them have been very limited over the years, I cannot express in words the amount of pure joy that I experienced being in their presence. It is truly rejuvenation even though I always knew that at the end of their visit I would experience great sadness from the ensuing separation. My heart breaks when I think that some parents face losing custody or are not allowed any contact with their children. Although this can be devastating, it doesn't have to be the end of your relationship with them. As a parent you can still continue to send love and blessings to your children. During this period of rejection by my son, I have continued to write him, but rather than sending it to him, I send it to a family member for safe keeping until he is ready to receive my letters. As noted in the introduction, any moment, any day could be my last, and I want my children to know the tremendous love I have for them. Also, change is constant, so what children aren't interested in reading today may be highly cherished tomorrow. In most cases maturity comes with age, so as a child grows their attitudes and concerns will adjust. Remember, access to your children may be in the control of another but write a letter as if it could be your very last opportunity. It's never too late to say, "I love you." Don't let your fears prevent this from happening. It is your decisions, not your conditions, which shape the future outcome of your life and theirs.

4

Growth on the Inside

"Just as your car runs more smoothly and requires less energy to go faster and farther when the wheels are in perfect alignment, you perform better when your thoughts, feelings, emotions, goals, and values are in balance."

– Brian Tracy (1944-)

An incarcerated parent has two choices of how they will deal with the reality of prison. They can continue their bad habits that contributed to the loss of their freedom and walk around with bitterness and anger, or they can see it as an opportunity to grow and make needed changes in their lives. I chose the latter. I chose to change. The more I thought about my past and future, I realized that I have to be the person first that I want my children to be. If I want them to be hard workers, rather than lecture to them, I have to be a hard worker. If I want them to show kindness and compassion towards others, then I have to consistently show kindness and compassion towards others. This may sound easy, but as previously stated, personal growth is painful. Change is painful. In growth comes true freedom. It has been my desire to be the absolute best dad that I can be, and I am determined to do it the best way I know how. No matter how I might fail from time to time, I will never stop trying.

I believe a truly intelligent person welcomes new ideas, and believes listening is more important than talking. Many people prefer to think with talking instead of listening. Only by listening can we absorb new ideas and possibilities. Ask questions instead of arguing or debating an issue. I think we all have potential and are blessed with skills. The one thing that often holds us back is our self-doubt or lack of confidence. Remember, failure is part of any process, but those who avoid failure also avoid eventual success. Do your best to get past the fears of failure and rejection. Do not bury your failures; get inspired by them. Parent with your actions, not your words. It took me many hours and lots of effort to get to where I am today. Early on in my sentence, I was aware of my many unresolved issues but avoided confronting my unresolved feelings. During my participation in a residential drug treatment program, I began to confront my attitudes, beliefs, and thinking processes. Down this road to freedom, I built upon each and every lesson I learned in the program. I also took this opportunity to participate in a Christ-based twelve-step recovery group called "Celebrate Recovery." In that step-study group, I really began to confront and share my emotional baggage and unresolved grief. The healing of my pain began.

For years, my unresolved emotions had been adversely affecting my moods, behaviors and thoughts. They had influenced my spiritual growth and impacted my healthy relationships with myself, others, and God. In twelve-step, I discovered many of what I refer to as character defects, such as: control issues, self-centeredness, and low self-worth. It's important as parents that we show our emotions in a healthy way. I began to see just how connected everything is and that I can't possibly be the best father I want to be until I deal with the emotions inside of me. I cannot express enough the tremendous value I received from participating in a twelve-step group. I became freed and discovered that I was not alone as a grieving parent or human being. Through my experience in the step-study work, I began to love myself and to feel valued and cherished. An awakening such as this, acted as a reminder of how limited my ability was to truly love others or allow them to love me prior to this change. We must love ourselves first in order to love others.

In our efforts to love our children, will our children keep their memories of us? How will the values we stood for, the love we shared, and the sacrifices we made along the way on their behalf be remembered? Will these memories leave them with feelings of pride or bitterness? Here are some of the most important values that I wish to live by every day of my life and pass on to my children: humility, wellness, financial freedom, family, integrity, spirituality, sensitivity, duty, relationships, responsibility, adventure, service, kindness, compassion, empathy, openness, forgiveness, and love.

Family relationships come in all shapes and sizes, but the bigger question is, "Are they whole or broken?" We have to be honest with ourselves when examining our own family relationships and whether or not they are healthy. We all deserve healthy connections to our families but especially with our children.

Our family influences who we are. Have you ever thought about your family and its origin? Did you grow up in an unhealthy family environment affected by addiction, criminal behaviors and mental health issues, or was your family healthy in body, mind and spirit? In either case, identifying behaviors that existed in our families will help give insight into ourselves.

I don't know about you, but my family had its share of dysfunction. Once again, I've learned through others sharing with me, self-study and self-examination that most families have their share of relationship problems. So, I know that I am not alone in sharing with you how difficult it has been to meet the challenges presented by rage, depression, addiction and criminal behavior in families. The only way to resolve a problem is through it. I can't tell you how much I have grown by going through a rigorous process of self-examination and self-reflection to help me face and transform painful and heart-breaking situations into functional and loving relationships within my own family.

The following lists are some examples of a family's "problem behaviors" and "positive behaviors" that you may want to consider for your self-examination and further reflection. The first step in resolving a family issue is to first identify it. What has been the impact of these problems on your current family structure and in your family of origin?

Problem Behaviors: Mental illness, depression, anger, resentment, criminal behavior, dishonesty, lack of faith, physical/emotional/sexual abuse, suicide, no sharing/closed off, not allowed to express feelings, workaholic, disrespect, and substance abuse/addiction.

Positive Behaviors: Prayer, having fun, willingness to forgive, sharing with others/openness, dependable, communication, allowed to express feelings, physical fitness, trustworthiness, closeness, self-worth, respect, faith, balanced life, and good health.

In addition, I found these following questions helpful during my self-examination process: How does your family operate? Do your family members trust each other? Does your family openly allow the expression of feelings? Does your family encourage growth and love?

There is no doubt that my past experiences have at times influenced my behavior which led to my incarceration. This in no way diminishes my responsibility of my actions. However, through careful self-examination it was made apparent that I must continue to confront my past in order to be successful in the future. I participated in the "Threshold" program which covered many facets of life to consider: managing mental and emotional health, decision making, personal relationships, accepting personal responsibility, daily living, wellness, continued educational growth, positive use of your time, and spiritual growth.

I cannot emphasize enough how important it is for you as a parent to examine yourself, self-reflect and attempt to confront these aspects of your life. Our children are observing us closely and taking mental notes. In order to have a healthy and successful relationship with our children, we must strengthen our foundation to its core. So, I encourage you to participate in any programs available to you that may cover these topics. If no programs are offered at your institution, I recommend searching your library, the psychology services library or any other resources that you may have access to. Let's take a closer look at the "facets of life" I previously mentioned. Please be honest with yourself while you respond to these questions for the benefit of yourself, your children and your family and friends.

Mental and Emotional Health: Are you actively managing or working on improving your mental health? What are some of your coping strategies? Are you acknowledging your feelings in a healthy way? Do you have a mentor, group, family member or friend that you can confide in?

Daily Life: What are your daily habits? Do you journal daily? Do you pray or meditate daily? Are you listening instead of talking? Do you try something new each day? Do you begin to right your wrongs?

Using Your Time Wisely: Are you balancing what you want to do versus what you have to do? Are you avoiding activities that were associated with your criminal behaviors? Are you focused on areas that will help you grow?

Accepting Responsibility: Have you accepted personal responsibility for your actions? Do you still blame someone else for your circumstances? Do you hold yourself accountable for your words, actions and thoughts?

Wellness: Do you physically take care of your body? Are you physically active and do you exercise regularly? Are you eating healthy foods and watching your diet? Are you getting enough rest?

Making Decisions: Do you consider the consequences prior to making your decisions? Do you seek advice from mentors, friends or family?

Continued Education: Do you challenge yourself each day to learn something new? Do you read books? Have you obtained your GED or High School Diploma? Do you have any interest in furthering your education, for example college course?

Relationships: Who are you choosing to spend your time with? What person has the single most influence in your life? Are your current relationships affecting your behaviors? If so, how – in a positive or negative manner? Are you attempting to rebuild trust with your children and or family members? Have you explored the dynamics of your family history in regard to healthy versus unhealthy relationships?

Spirituality: Do you pray or meditate? Do you have a higher power? What is your understanding of God? What is your definition of spirituality? Have you integrated these beliefs into your relationships?

We all must discover our purpose in life. If our goal is to be a better father, then we must practice self-reflection and self-examination of ourselves; consequently, we will discover what we need to change and in which direction to travel.

My purpose at this point in my life, in addition to be the best dad I can be, is to make sure I stay healthy mentally and physically in order to support my loved ones. If I'm not healthy, I'm of no benefit to anyone, especially my children.

We all will encounter problems along the way to discovering ourselves and our purpose in life. We must remember that problems are things that we can do something about. The problems we cannot solve are just a fact of life. We must see problems as opportunities. We must be enthusiastic and think positively about how to solve our problems. By using this mindset, I've been able to work through personal stressors, relationship changes, sickness and even deaths in my family.

In addition, I have experienced happy times, planned future adventures and discovered many new things about myself and the world. One of the biggest things that I've come to realize is that I must see things as they are and not how I want them to be. I encourage you to embrace these questions and take your time working through them as best and honestly as you can. You won't ever regret doing so, and the person you come to discover from your interior journey may be the parent you've always wanted for your children.

5

Discipline vs. Punishment

"No man can possibly improve in any company for which he has no respect enough to be under some degree of restraint."

– Lord Chesterfield (1694-1773)

As mentioned previously, prior to my arrest I played a very active role in my children's lives. They lived with me fifty percent of the time. At the time, I considered myself to be a fun-loving, protective, caring, and financially responsible father. It was only after my arrest and during my incarceration that much self-reflection took place. What I discovered was just how many areas in my life as a father needed improvement. Afterwards, I was consumed with shame and guilt. For one, I was shamed by the nature of my crime and second, I felt tremendous guilt for the way I punished my children by misunderstanding it as discipline. I did not know the difference then, but I do now.

During my first in person visit with my children, I explained how I had been wrong, and that I was very sorry and hoped they would find it in their hearts to forgive me. It was always amazing how full of love their hearts were and the loving responses they always gave me. I emphasized that the physical way I administered my punishment on them in the past was wrong. I realized by reflecting on my own experience as a boy that disciplining a child out of anger is wrong under any circumstance. I asked them to please promise me that they would never repeat this behavior with their own children in the ways that I had done. I made clear that there are many healthy alternatives.

Let's take a moment to discuss the aspects of discipline. I had sworn years earlier that I would never punish my children as I had been punished as a child. Now looking back, I did exactly the same thing without even being aware of it. I now see how much my unresolved anger masked a deeper underlying pain and how I was repeating a learned behavior from my father. As horrific as the prison experience has been, I am grateful that my parenting was interrupted by my arrest. It has given me the opportunity to evaluate huge swaths of my life and make the needed changes and improvements in order to become the father to my children that I always wanted for myself as a boy.

It seems to me that discipline and punishment are polar opposites in their administration and in their effects. Once again, the ancient lesson that one reaps what one sows applies to how we teach our children right from wrong, life's rules and roles, and appropriate boundaries and values. The primary objective for us as guides to our children is to cultivate our relationship with love and respect above all else. Discipline applied in reasonable, respectful, related, and reflective ways will help our children develop an internal code of values that will serve their needs and the needs of others for a lifetime and invite our children to reflect on their behavior and its consequences.

For example, your children are horse playing in the living room. Later your wife discovers a piece of broken glassware. She confronts the children and they both deny any involvement. When it's brought to your attention, rather than scolding them or responding with unchecked anger, you have a respectful discussion with them. You acknowledge that although accidents do happen, they must be responsible and hold themselves accountable for their actions. First, help your children clean up any remaining glass; second, have them write an age appropriate letter of apology to their mother; and finally, have them read or present the letter to their mother to encourage the taking of responsibility for their actions and to promote their being self-reflective in order to help them change their behaviors in the future.

On one hand, discipline offers guidelines and limits and teaches your children to problem solve, and to be responsible. Punishment, on the other hand, imposes an external set of rules that will not yield any long-lasting effect. In fact, it tends to promote deception and resentment by your children. What's more, punishment lowers self-worth, destroys self-control, and overwhelms your children with pain and fear.

As a boy, my dad told me to never climb a tree and that if I was caught, he would spank me. A few years later, despite my fears and risk of punishment, I decided to climb a tree with my friends and jump from it as they had done. Without the benefit of experience, I fell on my hands and knees, and then stopped my fall with my forehead. Although bruised, battered, and in pain, I kept my injury hidden from the pain of my father's disapproval and in fear of my punishment.

It's taken me years to overcome the humiliation, shame, fear, and pain I have suffered at the hands of my father through his learned ways of punishment, yet this does not compare to the shame I feel for how I've punished my children in ignorance. However, once I understood the difference between discipline and punishment, my relationship with my father and my children has changed every aspect of my life.

It's your job as a parent to guide and teach your children how to respect others and themselves and to use positive discipline that's age appropriate to accomplish this. There are additional reading resources recommended in the back of the book. Some of these will offer more detailed information and guidance. Just remember that regardless of the discipline you use, always tell your children that you still love them no matter what.

Healing, Forgiveness and Love

Love never gives up, love never loses faith, is always hopeful, and endures through every circumstance.

– 1 Corinthians 13:7

As a child, I grew up in a very rigid and authoritarian household. This is not to say that I was never hugged or verbally told, "I love you." However, I remember most often love being shown through physical punishment. My dad always took a moment after his anger calmed to explain the reasons for my punishment. He would make me sit next to him, oftentimes while I continued to sob, gasping for the next breath, and tell me that he had spanked me out of his love for me. Self-reflection and closer examination later in life revealed that I lived much of my life feeling flawed and defective as a son and human being. This hurt and low self-worth reached to my core. It became part of my identity. Like some traumatized children, I grew into an adult who lashed out like a wounded animal and very rarely said anything nice about anybody.

I understand now that many of my childhood experiences have contributed to many of my adulthood character flaws such as: perfectionism, striving for power and control, criticism and blame, judgmental and moralizing, patronization, and caretaking/helping others. All of these behaviors focused on someone else instead of myself. These early injuries also have surfaced in other ways such as anger, anxiety, fear, grief, and substance abuse. All of them were experienced well into my adult life. I experienced isolation and loneliness as well. I yearned for relationships, yet I hid from them. My loneliness extended itself even while in a crowd. Connecting to others when young was very difficult, yet today I love connecting with people. Rather than allow the fear to continue to rule me and cause me stay where I felt safest, I have spent many years confronting and climbing this mountain of pain.

Honesty has played a big role in my healing process. Being honest with myself and others is paramount while working any twelve-step program. It's easy to allow our damaged emotions to distort how we perceive those who have hurt us. While wounded, our perceptions are shaped by our feelings. For healing to occur, our perceptions must be brought into reality with truth. Two ways to accomplish our healing is to see those who hurt us as separate from what they did to us and to see ourselves as more than our wounded selves (victims). In working the twelve-steps, I first began to discover freedom from pain and guilt. I began to experience love for myself for the first time. The more I was able to love myself, the more I was able to love others.

Although I didn't realize it at the time, while working the twelve-steps and doing therapy with others, I was engaging in the healing process. The healing process is personal, unique to each individual, and involves a number of different aspects which need to be addressed during the healing process. I learned about this great process by reading Dr. Sidney and Suzanne Simon's book entitled: *Forgiveness: How to Make Peace with Your Past and Get on with Your Life* (1991). These particular issues in the healing process include, but are not limited to, the ways in which we were hurt, by whom we were hurt, by how we reacted to our hurt, by how we perceived those experiences, by what we came to believe about ourselves as a result of our hurt, by how we continue to interpret our hurt's effect on our lives, by the emotional support we receive, and by what we want our lives to become after surviving our hurt.

We all move through this process differently, but our end goal is the same: to improve our lives and attain peace of mind. Regardless of where we differ on our journeys and the time frame involved, we all will at times pass through six stages of healing. Keep in mind that these do not occur in order. Our steps may be small or large, and we may move forward or backward depending on our circumstances. The process is not without pain, but if you are tired of hurting and want peace within yourself, it's all worth the work. I am grateful once again to Dr. Sidney B. and Suzanne Simon for providing me with the following stages:

The first stage is "Denial." I have lived most of my life in this stage. I played down my painful past experiences and buried my thoughts and feelings about those experiences.

The second stage is "Self-Blame." This is a stage where we try to explain what happened by thinking we are somehow responsible. This wreaks havoc on our self-worth, and we find ourselves thinking that had we only done or acted differently, none of this would have happened. Even to this day, I find myself blaming myself at times for a wrong done to me that was clearly not my fault, then or now.

The third stage is the "Victim Stage." This is also a stage that I am all too familiar with. I recognized that I did not deserve any of the past hurt I had received and realized how those hurts damaged me as a person. Instead of healing my hurt, I exploited the victim card, wallowed in self-pity, overindulged at the expense of others, and lashed out at anyone who may have crossed me.

The fourth stage is "Indignation." While in this stage, I was angry at those who hurt me and at the world. My thoughts concluded that those who have hurt me deserve to suffer just as I have. I had little to no tolerance for others and my self-righteousness soared.

The fifth stage is "The Survivor Stage." At this stage, I realized that although hurt, I had survived. Although my past was indeed a painful experience that took from me, it has also given me insights and wisdom. Consequently, I have become valued, strong, compassionate, able to laugh and smile, and be interested in many things beyond the pain itself. I also realized that I have done the best that I could.

The sixth stage is "Integration." I have come to the realization that the people who have hurt me in my past may have been doing the best that they could at the time, that I am more than my pain, and they are more than the person who injured me. By acknowledging this, I can release the hold I have on them and use that energy to focus on more positive things. I can put the past in perspective without forgetting it while still letting go of the pain and my excess emotional baggage.

I mentioned earlier in the book that my relationship with my mother is probably the best now that it has ever been. I want you to know that it has not been without much work, challenges, and painful experiences. Approximately one year prior to my being rejected by my son, I became enraged at my mother's continued denial of a family secret. I wrote my mom a letter in which I expressed my anger and discontent. I informed her that I no longer wanted her in my life, and I would live life on my own. I thought at the time that the pain was too much to bear and it would be easier to just cut ties.

The timing of my anger towards my mom came as I was in the middle of working the twelve-steps. I was trying to confront years of unresolved pain. Now looking back, I see that at the time I was bouncing around the different stages of healing. I was trying to find my way. After cutting off my mom, I continued to work the steps, searching for inner peace and resolve. Over time, my mother and I began to resume brief communication. When my son rejected me, it sent shock waves down my spine. I immediately realized the immense pain my mom must have endured from my rejection of her.

During a subsequent phone call with her, I shared my regret and remorse for the things I had said to her. She explained that the words had indeed been painful, but it was water under the bridge and that it did not change her love for me one bit. Since then, we both have grown within ourselves and in our relationship. My mother's actions were great examples of unconditional love and forgiveness.

Many people forego making the decision to forgive others. It can be very painful to open up a dreadful box of pain, forcing us to relive unpleasant experiences and admit to ourselves how badly we were hurt in the past. Opening up leaves us very vulnerable, and it can be downright frightening. It's easier to avoid than face our fears. By not doing so, we can use the pain as an excuse for everything that is wrong in our lives. We can claim it as the reason why we are the way we are. Another excuse not to forgive is that we can continue to be one of the good guys. After all, the bad guys were the ones who hurt us. Not forgiving also gives us a sense of power that we didn't feel when we were being hurt by others. And, of course, not forgiving protects us from being victims again by those who have hurt us in the past or even new people in our lives. Holding on to our pain keeps our guard up against being rejected, betrayed, deceived, or otherwise. After a close self-examination, one can easily see how the lack of forgiveness is an emotional barrier to any healthy relationship.

Working the twelve-steps helped me with the ability to begin forgiving others for hurting me. It also helped me make amends when possible and appropriate with those I've hurt in the past. Some might say, "I can't ever forget so I can't forgive." We may never be able to forget some of life's painful experiences, but we can choose to forgive. Forgiving is a personal choice, a decision that must be made by us. It doesn't happen overnight. It's a process. We don't have to wait on the other person. Grudges only hurt those holding on to them. Haven't you ever heard the expression that holding onto resentment is like drinking poison and waiting for the other person to die? Forgiving another is liberation from anger, resentment, and the quest for vengeance that can eat away at us, eventually destroying us.

Getting rid of these pent up emotions is a joyful and beautiful experience. It opens your heart, allows your consciousness to expand, and makes us feel more connected to ourselves, others, and life itself. It hasn't been easy for me to forgive people who have hurt me in the past, but I wanted to be free from the chains that bound me to anger, hostility, and bitterness. At the same time, I have been able to examine the many hurts that I have caused others over the years. It's my prayer that they will all one day be able to forgive me.

I mentioned in chapter 3 about receiving a letter from my teenage son and that I would discuss my response to him. I shared with you the great pain that I experienced while reading his letter. I decided to share it with a small group of trusted men who were part of my twelve-step recovery group. It was very tough for me to read the words aloud. I remember seeing grown men cry by the time I reached the conclusion. I know that with pain comes growth and with growth comes healing. The letter caused great turmoil within me. While my son struggled with me as a father, I in turn was struggling with the memories of my own father. With feelings of rejection by my son overwhelming me, I began to realize how I had previously rejected my mom and my dad. My own actions had come full circle. I was seeing a reflection of myself in my own son. Are we really two persons or just a continuation of each other? We are definitely linked and there cannot be an understanding of one without an understanding of the other. My initial response to my son was one of hurt, confusion, and defensiveness without taking time to reflect.

A couple of questions emerged that I had to ask myself. How can I be more loving in this situation? And what wisdom can I learn from this experience? During this critical thought process, I came up with what I considered to be a proper and final response: I needed to honor my son's wishes. I needed to love him without conditions. I took this thought to a dear friend to discuss it more in depth.

During my discussion with my friend, we looked at the subject of love and what it truly means. No words can encompass it all, but I can describe some of how I now experience love. Love does not want or fear anything. It gives without expecting in return. It is to see a person as they are and not what we want them to be. Love does not discriminate. I like to think of it as a beautiful flower. A flower does not choose some and not allow others to enjoy its fragrance. It gives to all. Love has patience. It is not self-seeking. Love is not easily angered and keeps no record of rights or wrongs. It always hopes, perseveres, and never fails. It just is.

After our discussion, I composed a final letter to my son. I sent a copy to his mother, asking that she please make sure he read it. I explained that although I was deeply saddened about our loss of further communication, I understood and respected his feelings. I informed him that nothing he could ever do or say will ever diminish my love for him. I explained that love is patient, love is kind, love isn't dependent on anything being a certain way that it just is, that I would honor his request, and that my heart will remain open to his no matter what he decides. When the day he may return arrives, I will be here to greet him with open arms. No matter what has happened or will happen, I will always be here for him.

One of the things we have to eventually do as parents is let go of seeing our children as an extension of ourselves. As parents, we want to fix and solve everything for our children. Sending this letter to my son and letting go of my want for him was the most difficult act that I have ever faced as a father. I realized that for my son's sake, I had to stop operating from meeting my needs and to put my son's needs first. I had to put down my agenda and move over so eventually he will be free to express his wishes and responses to any situation, and I can receive them without the need to fix or change anything. I had to allow him to grow into an independent person and accept responsibility for his own choices.

I struggle with the decision to allow my son the freedom to grow and learn from his decisions to cut off communication with me. Not a day goes by that I don't think about him and how he's doing. But with support from friends, family, support groups, prayer, and my desire for the best outcome, I've managed to accept reality as it is, not as I want it to be. I'm a different man and father than I once was. It's not just about me and my needs anymore. It's about being love itself. I don't know about you, but I am happiest when I'm giving love. It's my belief that all we want is to love and be loved. It's the giving of love that's often the hardest to grasp.

7

Communication

"Deep listening is miraculous for both listener and speaker. When someone receives us with open-hearted, non-judging, intensely interested listening, our spirits expand."

– Sue Patton Thoele

Our communication with our children is very important. Since most incarcerated parents mostly communicate via letters and phone calls, it's especially important for us to get it right when presented with the opportunity to connect with them. Communication is a requirement of all healthy relationships. Our most vital skill in communication is active listening.

In active listening, we do not have to offer up a solution. We simply let our children know-that we understand how they are feeling. We acknowledge their feelings in a variety of ways. Being a good active listener takes work, effort, and sensitivity in order to understand our children's feelings. When listening to your children, try your best to be open-minded. Disregard your own beliefs and views at least temporarily. I feel the most important thing that we can do as parents is to carefully listen to what our children have to share. Remember, they are constantly communicating their needs to us in verbal and non-verbal ways.

Through trial and error, we all have learned, "words will never hurt me" isn't true. In fact, words do hurt and can hurt us deeply. Misspoken words can hurt our children even more deeply. No one wants to be bombarded with negativity or a parent being ultra-critical of them. We can harness the positive power of words and put them to work in our children's lives. We simply start by being more mindful about what we are saying, how we are saying it, and what effect it is having on our children and ourselves. We can choose to speak of inspiration, love, gratitude, and health in more healing ways. By doing so, we are transforming, improving, and making progress within our children and ourselves. We reveal ourselves by sharing our thoughts and feelings. When speaking to my children, I always make a concerted effort to continually affirm their worth and potential. I also enjoy giving them praise. I do my best to stay positive, upbeat, energetic, and completely interested in all that they are willing to share. Even when the message to be delivered is difficult, I choose my words, tone, and attitude wisely.

After hundreds of calls, I have learned that no two phone calls will be the same. Our children get tired or have bad days just like we do. During these times, they may have less to say, or they may be less engaged. On these occasions, do your best to understand their feelings, stay positive, and reassure them that things will be okay. Sometimes when I find myself on one of these calls, I've learned to make small talk and ask about things that I know they are interested in. For example, "What do you have planned during your Spring break?" or, "What's your current favorite video game?"

Always remember to be respectful when speaking with your children and to others who may be within reach of your conversation. This applies whether you are on the phone or in a visiting room area. I cannot tell you the countless times that I have apologized to my children for the guy next to me on the phone who is saying offensive and inappropriate things for children to hear. Without respect for one another, there can be no meaningful communication.

Keep in mind that good communication extends beyond your children. This includes friends, family, and especially our children's mom/dad or their respective caregiver. By being respectful and polite we can appropriately avoid unnecessary conflicts with others. Good communication encourages problem-solving, settling disagreements, and getting our needs met appropriately. During my time incarcerated, I have learned that my available phone time is valuable and limited; therefore, my phone time must be utilized to the fullest and as productive as possible.

I now realize how I failed in effective communication with my son. When I felt as though his mother and I weren't communicating effectively, I expressed my frustration to him, and he may have interpreted my comments as blaming not only his mother, but him. Instead of putting my son in the middle, I should have expressed my concerns to his mother directly. After much self-reflection and study, I eventually was able to do so. After expressing my concerns to her in a respectful and patient tone, I was able to get the information I needed without involving my son.

Furthermore, another failure in communication that still pains me to this day is how some of my letters may have emotionally affected my son. I shared too much personal information too soon. Looking back now, I realize that he was too young to process the level of my disclosure. I can only imagine how overwhelming this must have been for him. Don't get me wrong. I am not encouraging you to not share yourself or not be honest with your children. The key, in my view, is that our communication must not only be honest, but it also must be age appropriate in order to meet our children's needs, not our own.

In my efforts to maintain our bond as a father and son, and rather than focusing on my son's needs alone, I treated him more like a friend, expecting him to meet my needs while I met his. As a result, he became overwhelmed and inappropriately responsible for meeting his father's needs. This is important to know so you don't make the same mistakes as I have done. If you are unsure whether a certain disclosure or information is age appropriate to your children, don't hesitate to communicate and consult with a fellow father, counselor, pastor, or friend.

8

Being Involved With Your Children

"Do what you can, with what you have, where you are."

– Theodore Roosevelt (1858-1919)

Being involved with your children offers you a chance to be positive, be a role model, and to effect positive change in your children's lives. There are a number of reasons that are very important for us as parents to remain active and involved in our children's lives even though we may be incarcerated. As parents, we always want to do what's best for our children. They need us in their lives regardless of what we may be thinking. Being separated physically from our children makes being involved with them even more challenging. Nonetheless, we can get and stay involved in some fashion with our continued efforts. By staying active in our children's lives, we can help make a number of positive contributions. Let's look more closely at some of these.

EMOTIONS

As discussed earlier in the book, oftentimes we find that we have to make changes in ourselves first before we can contribute to the well-being of our children. Change in ourselves requires us to make a commitment to do so. It also requires us to put forth our effort, and of course, it takes time. Always try to choose your words and actions carefully. Never use manipulation in an attempt to affect your children's emotions.

More importantly, do not use tactics such as shame, pity, or guilt to garner your child's attention. Our children watch what we say and do, always! Put them first in your life. It is not just about us any longer. First, get in touch with your mood, feelings, and emotions, and second, don't be afraid to openly share your emotions with your children. By doing so, you are showing them by example that it's okay to express feelings. Wow! What a way to draw close and bond with your child. Your children will be less likely to have emotional or behavioral problems as a result. Imagine the relief they must feel to know that whenever talking with mom or dad, they will listen with understanding. I think a moment such as this is equivalent to a long-distance hug. I remember on more than one occasion; I've spoken with my children on the phone and allowed them to openly express their thoughts and feelings which gave them a sense of being heard and honored. My intention was not to judge or criticize, but to listen and be available to meet their needs.

Furthermore, be sure to pay attention to your attitude and tone when communicating with your children. If you have had a bad day, choose another time to call them. By doing so, your conversation will be less likely to be confrontational and aggressive and more likely to be positive and upbeat. If at all possible, always speak to your children with sincerity and in a loving way.

Always show your love in whatever way you can, whether it be in phone calls, letters, or visits. We may not be able to close the physical distance with our children, but we can definitely close the emotional distance.

RELATIONSHIPS

Relationships with our children mean everything to them. Our children want us to make time for them and take an interest in their lives. They want to be loved and hear us say that we love them. They want our actions to relay love to them. It is up to us to help guide them as they grow and to help them make their own good decisions about relationships. As fathers, our views will greatly influence how our children may see others when it comes to relationships. They will closely watch or listen to how we treat others. I taught my children at a very early age to treat others as they would like to be treated. I have continued to emphasize this as they have grown. By treating others with humility, kindness, and compassion, they will be making this world a better place. I want to maintain the best possible relationship with my children so that they will feel safer and more confident and so that they will be less likely to abuse alcohol and drugs or engage in other self-destructive behaviors.

What's more, a parent's love and communication with their children becomes the catalyst for the health and well-being of all other relationships in their lives. For example, a child who knows that things are good with mom/dad has one less thing to worry about while at school or at home. Our ultimate wish as parents is that our children will stay out of trouble altogether and learn how to develop healthy relationships for themselves. By keeping a positive and healthy relationship with our children, this will hopefully transfer over not only to their mother or primary caregiver, but to everyone they meet. For all parents, it is very important not only to respect your children but also to respect their other parent or guardian. Whether you are married or not, keeping a good relationship with the children's mother is vital. In order to avoid bringing up past conflicts and disagreements, stay focused on the children and their needs first. Even in those situations where you don't get along, continue to show respect for your children's sake.

Don't forget to have fun being a parent. Being a good parent isn't all gloom and doom, even if incarcerated. Laugh often but keep your humor positive and be consciously aware of your children's feelings. I like to sometimes ask my children, "Anything funny happen lately?" Sometimes they respond with a recent event that occurred at school. Also, we have shared laughs, games, and activities during visits when we were able to interact and bond. Our visits may have been short, but they were amazing and fun while they lasted. Those moments will always be cherished and remain memories for us to share in the future.

FAITH AND SPIRITUALITY

"If God brings you to it,
He will bring you through it.
In Happy moments, praise God.
In Difficult moments, seek God.
In Quiet moments, worship God.
In Painful moments, trust God.
In Every moment, thank God."

– Anonymous (Muslim quote)

I have found my faith in God and my spirituality to be key ingredients in my daily life to help me in difficult times. I have taken full advantage of opportunities to pray, meditate, read, learn, and take programs both inside and outside the institution through correspondence. I have shared my faith and beliefs with my children throughout the years. It is my desire that they have seen my growth and optimism and will apply the same to their daily lives. One thing I've always shared with my children is prayer. We don't do this on every phone call, but from time to time we pray together. I have given them the opportunity to lead us in prayer and at times they have accepted. Those moments are both special and memorable.

I've always chosen to believe that there is a God and that we as individuals must always try to make the best possible decisions. We need values and some type of positive belief system. We need to know the difference between right and wrong. I've tried to instill these same values in my children when they were young by attending church with them as much as possible. It's one attribute and foundation that I can be proud of today. However, I failed myself miserably and lost sight of practicing goodness and values in my own life.

The Bible is full of stories of pain and failure by human beings. These traits have been with us since the beginning. Some are worse than others, but all indicate the brokenness and flaws in our humanity. Our free choice and intentions to do what's right makes the difference in the end. God specializes in broken people and wants to make all of us whole again.

Even though I'm physically imprisoned, I've found freedom. Freedom resides in my heart. I've gone from loneliness and hostility to acceptance and love. I now see reality for what it is rather than what I want it to be. I see prayer and meditation as a way to talk and listen to God, putting my faith in something bigger and more powerful than myself. It's my way to let go and let God.

I no longer see God as some guy sitting upstairs looking down at me. What a disconnect. It's unfortunate that I experienced such separation from God for so many years. I now see Him and His love as an extension of me and my love. After all, God is love. We are one, and I am united in His fullness within me. Together, we are part of everything. As a matter of fact, we are all connected and part of a bigger whole. Seeing God in this way allows my love to flow naturally and because of this my heart is open and available to others. My consciousness is able to expand which allows me to feel more connected to myself, others, and the Source of life itself. As a result, my relationships have become more stable and loving, my mental and physical health has improved, and more doors have opened to new opportunities. I have a sense of purpose, know what's most important in life, and am aware of my own mortality. I feel more confident and in control of my actions, behaviors, and thoughts. I feel much happier and my emotions are consistently more positive. All of the above allow me to be a really healthy example for my children.

It's my prayer that my children merely use me as a guide ultimately to discover for themselves the type of relationship I currently have with God. I look forward to sharing with them that God is already within us. Although sometimes beneficial, church membership is not required. Like all truths, they must discover them in their own way, in their own time, and on their own journey.

I encourage you to seek your own path towards spirituality. I encourage you to share it with your children. You'd be surprised how much they will model their lives after yours and just how many questions they may present to you about your spiritual journey. It's a great opportunity for them to grow and for you to enhance your relationship with them. Just remember, be respectful of their beliefs and don't try to force your religious beliefs on them. Keep a positive attitude while accepting your daily struggles and work through your difficult emotions. This is all part of your spiritual growth.

PHYSICAL HEALTH

Although we may not be there physically with our children, we can still discuss the importance of a healthy lifestyle, including eating healthy foods such as fruits and vegetables. It is important for us to monitor our own lifestyle, such as rest, exercise, and eating habits since our children closely watch what we do. They may be less likely to take our advice seriously if we are overweight and in poor physical condition. Besides, don't you want to be around to see your future grandchildren? If you cannot find the strength to do it for yourself, then do it for your children.

I remember sharing my efforts to eat well and increase my physical activity with my son. During our discussions, I emphasized working out. My son replied, "Dad! I don't need to diet." He took my emphasis on working out as just weight loss however, my intent was to relay to him the importance of being physically fit and choosing to eat healthy foods when given the opportunity.

ROLE MODEL

Some incarcerated parents allow their past actions to define them. Sometimes they even continue the same criminal behavior while in prison. Don't be one of those parents. Our past actions do not have to define us. Everyone has made a bad choice in life, but now is our chance to shine for our children. Now is your chance to create a new healthy lifestyle and share it with them. Show them that change within ourselves is possible. Show them that although incarcerated, we can overcome the challenges we face in a positive way. This will be one of the best lessons that we could ever teach our children. What a way to show your courage during times of adversity.

Three characteristics that I try to live up to each day are: kindness, which includes how I am with myself as well as with others; compassion, which also includes me as well as others; and gratitude, which means being thankful for all I have and all that I have to give. We can show our children that we are willing to accept responsibility for our past behaviors. Let's even go a step further by holding ourselves accountable for what we haven't done as parents. We need to stop the blaming of everyone or everything else. By taking responsibility for what we've done and who we are, we will provide another great lesson for our children to learn by watching us. This will show great courage on our part.

Furthermore, we can model for our children the value of an education by taking several classes that are offered to us while in prison. We will then be able to share what we've learned and have related discussions with our children. Maybe we can further our education by enrolling in college courses made available? Our initiative to educate ourselves will show our efforts and this may inspire our children to do well in school. Our interest in a particular subject may lead them to a greater interest in that same discipline.

In addition to showing our children how to be accountable and responsible for their own growth, we must be men/women of our word. We must do what we say we will do. If we tell our children that we are going to write or call them, then by all means, make every effort to do so. Let's show them that they can depend on us. Let's show them what it means to be a reliable parent, a dependable human being. This will go a long way in building a trusting relationship with them. Every time we take a chance by reaching out to them, we raise the bar on how they see us.

If the opportunity presents itself, you may want to discuss with your children's caregiver or another family member the possibility of finding a mentor for your children. Successful mentoring requires everybody involved to support the idea. Mentors often include friends of the family, neighbors, or church members who are caring and willing to volunteer their time to your children. A number of mentoring programs in the community include either faith based or non-profit organizations. Many of these may cater to families with incarcerated parents.

The time spent with a mentor can be time well spent with your children. Your children will have the opportunity to talk about everyday choices and even discuss their future goals and vision with the mentor. What's more, your children may be given the opportunity to participate in activities or attend events that otherwise would be unavailable to them. Remember, mentors cannot replace your role as a parent; however, they can help support your children in ways not available to you as you continue to do your part staying connected to your children while in prison.

Our children learn the most from us by what we do, not by what we say; therefore, we must practice what we preach. It does no good to express concerns to our children about a specific behavior when we continue to do the opposite. This is confusing to our children. If we have bad habits, we need to replace them with positive ones. I must be true to the values that I practice and want to pass on to my children. The following is a list of values I currently embrace and wish to instill in my children by example: explore; discover and dream big; be fair to yourselves and others; respect people; listen to others - sometimes they can see things you cannot; enjoy life; play; have fun; work hard, but have fun while doing so; believe in God; believe in yourself; love your family; respect your spouse-partner-or significant other; do what's right not what's popular; be humble; live; laugh; love; and always cherish your children.

What values do you currently embrace? What values do you want to pass on to your children? Perhaps the following questions will help you clarify and define what values you wish to model and instill in your children by your good example:

1. What do you stand for as a parent?
2. Do you have morals or standards?
3. What do you consider your rights and wrongs?
4. Do you allow God to influence your decisions?

9

What Children Need and Want

"Respect is not fear and awe; it ... is the ability to see a person as he is, to be aware of his unique individuality. Respect, thus, implies the absence of exploitation. I want the loved person to grow and unfold for his own sake, and in his own ways, and not for the purpose of serving me."

– Eric Fromm (1900-1980)

Can we agree that we all have needs, especially our children? Three of the top needs are: to be wanted, to be needed, and to be respected.

TIME

As incarcerated parents, one thing that is very valuable to us is our time. We realize no matter how hard we may try, we cannot create more of it. Each day we are incarcerated, we realize that we will never get back the prior day, week, or year. Being an active parent and meeting the needs in our children's lives requires us to give some of our time. It requires us to give ourselves. Focusing our attention on our children is the most important way we can relay our love to them. What better way to communicate to them that they are valued, cherished, and loved beyond measure. We are giving up our time for the benefit of our children and the best time to love them is always now!

PRAISE

Do you ever give your children praise when talking with them or in your letters written to them? I don't know about you, but I love getting praise even to this day. I know our children love getting it, too, especially from their parents. I cannot give my children enough praise, not just praise for doing the right thing, but praise for just being themselves. Sometimes I give my children praise for the simplest things. It's my way to use positive reinforcement and encouragement. For example, when my son informed me that he was rinsing the dishes in order to load the dishwasher, I praised him for doing a thorough job. On another occasion, he informed me that he was folding the clean laundry so it could be put away. I immediately gave him praise for his thoughtfulness and willingness to help his mom with the chores. I emphasized that his efforts showed him to be a responsible young man. Not only does this type of praise feel great to our children, but it helps build their confidence. They feel a sense of self-satisfaction, self-worth, and appreciation.

OUR CHILDREN'S FREEDOM

Our children need us to allow them to grow and change. I feel that it's important that we allow our children to ultimately choose their own path in life. We cannot and should not try to mold our children into ourselves or anyone else for that matter. We have to allow them to be free and discover themselves. That's probably one of the greatest gifts we can give as a parent.

Our children need us to trust them and know that they will do their best not to let us down. They need to be believed in and that includes everything about them. They need encouragement versus criticism, and they need us to let them handle things unless they ask for help.

I continually encourage my children to follow their dreams. I constantly affirm their self-worth by letting them know I believe in them and that they can achieve anything they set out to do. I have communicated to them many times that I love and accept them no matter what. There is no specific thing that they ever have to do to earn my love.

STAGES OF DEVELOPMENT

Before we discuss other ideas to interact with our children, I want to briefly mention the developmental stages of our children. The stages have been provided in the appendix as a reference for you to use. Please keep in mind they are only a guide for you as a parent. Treat them as indicators of their growth and the milestones they reach. Each child is unique, different, and may act outside their stages from time to time. Your awareness of these stages will provide them with what your children need to thrive. More importantly, it will prevent any undue frustration that arises from unrealistic expectations. Don't let this worry you. Just be aware and enjoy watching your children grow into happy, healthy, and well-adjusted adults (see appendix).

OUR CHILDREN'S INTEREST

Do you pay attention to your children's interests or hobbies? What about their favorite class at school, or their choice in music? Every child is unique and different. For example, one of my children has a great interest in law enforcement and the military. The other is currently interested in outdoor activities and online gaming. Because of this, I sought out magazine subscriptions that were related to their interests. I sent them magazines on gaming, fishing, and police work. On occasion, I have asked my son what his favorite book was so that I could order it. After reading his favorite book, we were able to discuss our favorite passages and how the story affected us. As you can see, all the above examples are ways for a parent to show interest in their children's lives and opens the door for more and more connections with them. We need to know what our children like.

In fact, I have experienced some great connections with my children when they shared their favorite songs with me. Over the years, I have watched their choice of music go from one extreme to another. Their favorite songs today are a far cry from just a couple years ago. During a phone conversation, I recall my son suggested a popular song in order to elicit my response. After I listened to it, we enjoyed another opportunity to bond with each other. I love hearing about their interests and sharing in their lives with them. As parents, we need to continue to look for ways to connect with our children through their interests.

If you haven't already done so, it's time to show your children that you really care. At least try to become an expert on your children's interests. Learn as much as you can. Take time to find out all the exciting things that are happening in their lives. The more interest you show, the more they will share. Here are some things I feel you as a parent should already know or at least make an attempt to discover about your children.

1. Birthdate and plans for celebration?
2. Favorite Hobbies?
3. Interests?
4. Favorite Sports and Teams?
5. If participating in sports and position played?
6. Favorite song, artist, group, or genre?
7. Favorite shows or movies?
8. Favorite books?
9. Favorite colors?
10. Favorite animals?
11. Favorite places?
12. Best friend(s)?
13. Favorite subjects and teachers at school?
14. Favorite video games?
15. Likes and dislikes?
16. Dreams and goals?
17. Girlfriend, boyfriend, or crushes?
18. When they are happiest?
19. How can you support them better as a parent?
20. What do they need from you as a parent?

According to Dr. Kevin Leman in his book Planet Middle School, the top complaints from middle-aged children are that we as parents do not understand them or the world they live in, that we do not listen, that we are only concerned with things like taking care of chores, and that we are not around or are unavailable to talk to them when needed. If we have an open line of communication and healthy relationship with our children, we can ask questions that will allow them to tell us about their world. If we practice active listening, they will know that we find great importance in what they have to say. We may be restricted from being physically present due to our incarceration. However, we can be present emotionally, which means everything to them.

During my years of incarceration, I have tried nearly every imaginable way possible to stay actively involved in my children's lives. Staying connected to them has been a priority of mine. How can it not be the priority of any attuned, attentive parent? An incarcerated parent's usual contact with their children includes visits, phone calls, letters, and other personalized activities. These various ways or styles of contact enhance our relationship with our children. They also reassure our children of our love for them and that we are doing okay as parents. Every expression of love indicates to our children that we have spent our time thinking of them. We've previously discussed the importance of active listening and communication as well as age appropriate letters. So, the majority of our focus below will be on additional activities that you can do to stay actively involved in your children's lives.

VISITS

Visits with my children are some of the most memorable moments during my incarceration. I always purchased photo tickets in advance. My children were always extremely excited to see me. Sometimes, to be honest, I think they enjoyed the vending machines a bit more than me. They often couldn't get enough hugs and kept their arms around me or hands touching mine most of the entire visit. Hugs are amazing and, in my opinion, we can never give our children too many. I stayed positive, made eye contact and tried to keep a smile. It was always mind blowing and amazing how much they had grown since I had last seen them. They were chatter boxes most of the visit, and I enjoyed listening to every single moment. When given the opportunity, I was sure to ask about different aspects of their lives. In fact, most times my mother and I got to catch up on very little. However, my mom enjoyed watching our interaction, knowing that she had helped make these special moments possible. We were able to enjoy playing games together and on more than one occasion, we divided up our food so each of us got to try different things. I thoroughly enjoyed those moments of sharing and so did they. On a few occasions, we shed a few tears together. Those were emotional moments and provided opportunities for me to reassure them that everything would be okay. I was able to tell them during those times that it's okay to cry, and it is okay to express your feelings. The end of our visits was always the most difficult. I did not want to see them go, nor did they want to leave.

I knew, once I watched them walk out that door, I would experience that all too common feeling that a part of me was now missing. Regardless of the sadness that followed, the visits offered me a sense of hope and renewed strength just by being reminded that I was the father of these two amazing and wonderful boys.

Please don't take the sharing of my visits as being boastful. Although they were pleasant and memorable, there was sadness involved. Visits with any family members, especially our children, need preparation and planning. Every parent has unique circumstances with children of different ages. Visits can be very unpredictable and quite emotional for everyone involved. A parent must mentally and emotionally prepare himself for the unexpected and remain calm no matter the outcome. Some children may cry or scream. Some may be stand-offish or reluctant to engage and others may be very clingy. Your children's age will play a role in their behavior, as well as the previous level of bonding that has been established. It's important as parents to be patient, calm, open-minded, and positive during your interaction with your children at visits. Understand that your family or children may be tired from the travel or waiting to enter the facility. They may be frightened or even embarrassed by their surroundings. Be reassuring, smile, and let them know just how grateful you are that they have come to spend time with you.

Prepare for the many emotions you may experience during your visit, and most certainly be prepared for the afterwards. The sadness or loneliness that you may experience is normal and may challenge your self-worth or validity as a parent. Just know that you have done the best you could do in the situation. Hopefully your visit will be a success and there will be many more to follow.

PHONE CALLS

I've learned through experience that the expense of our phone calls while incarcerated can range from costly to outrageous. Because of the invaluable gifts and joy that hearing our children's voices brings and the reassurance of hearing your voice brings them, you may want to utilize whatever service available to reduce the cost of this priceless opportunity to show your love to your children. Regardless of your financial limitations, any time spent talking with your children is better than none. Hearing your voice means everything to them, and it is one sure way to relieve their fear that you are indeed okay and that you care. So, call when given the opportunity, however short it may be. Especially try to call on birthdays or other special occasions. My most memorable phone calls were calling my children each and every birthday to sing "Happy Birthday" to them.

LETTERS

Letters are very important to our children. Although I may have received very few letters from my children over the years, I cherished each and every one of them. I've questioned myself in regard to the amount and frequency of letters that I've sent to my children. After years of writing, my son informed me during a conversation that he had kept every letter that I had ever sent him. Hearing him say that meant the world to me.

In my letters, I always expressed my love for them. I have tried to stay positive and discuss topics they would find interesting. I asked about their lives and praised them for accomplishments. As I mentioned previously, I now see that I may have shared some negative emotions that my son was just not ready to interpret at his age. Be sure to read your letter over before sending it. You may also want to consult with a friend or mentor prior to sending your letter.

QUESTION AND ANSWER LETTERS

I remember sending a "question and answer" letter to my children during my time away. My mother was able to help make sure my children answered, and she ensured their responses were put in the mail to me. I have looked at those letters and their answers many times over the years, often bringing tears. Each time I read their responses, I am reminded of just how much they love me and how incredibly fortunate I am to be their father. Although their responses are very personal, in an effort to encourage you to seek similar invaluable responses from your children, I'd like to share my letters with you (see appendix).

WRITE A POEM

I'll be the first to admit that I won't win any awards as a poet. However, this hasn't stopped me from writing poems for my children. As an inspiration to incarcerated parents and to memorialize the poems for my sons, I'd like to share them with you (see appendix).

WRITE A BOOK

Have you ever considered writing a book for your children or better yet, writing it with them? Knowing their interests may help you narrow down your topic of choice. What's fun and exciting about writing stories together is that each person can create their own story and ultimately their own ending. For example, you start out the story and mail it to your child for them to continue it. Instruct them to use their imagination and have fun while writing, and then have them mail it back to you when they are ready so that you can continue the story. Who knows what you may discover about each other by sharing this project?

PHOTOS

On a few occasions over the years, I have purchased photo tickets so that I could have photos taken in order to send home to my children. It's a great way to let them see I'm doing okay. One picture is worth a thousand words. I always love receiving photos from them as well. If your children or their caregiver are unwilling or unable to send you photographs, you could reach out to a family member or friend to see if they can assist you. In the age of social media, a family member or friend could access your children's photos with their caregiver's permission. If nothing else, you could draw a self-portrait and encourage your children to do the same.

DRAWINGS

My artistic skill could use some improvement when it comes to drawing any type of picture, but it hasn't stopped me from trying. My son has drawn me a few things over the years. I did my best to return the favor. I've drawn him a race car as well as a few depictions of his favorite animal, the wolf. Use your imagination. Maybe you have your children draw something and you color the picture or vice versa. The most important aspect of this activity is that your children and you are sharing yourselves, your creativity, and your love for each other.

COLORING BOOKS

There are some really cool coloring books out on the market these days: superheroes, race cars, sports teams, animals, and everything else imaginable. Check with your local commissary to see if colored pencils or crayons are available for you to purchase. If not, maybe you can participate in arts and crafts in order to gain access to these utensils. After you color a specific picture, you can cut out the page and mail it to your children or maybe you prefer to complete the entire book before mailing it. Either way, it's your personal touch that will be appreciated and perhaps treasured.

ART AND CRAFTS

Another activity that can be enjoyed by parents is participating in any available arts and crafts programs. For example, I enrolled in a stick art program and made my children and others various items depicting their favorite sports teams' logos. These items were well received and hopefully cherished. Beading is another popular craft. I've watched others make some amazing jewelry and bracelets to both sell and send home to their loved ones. Other crafts include cross-stich and crocheting. One fellow inmate showed me an amazing cross-stich Christmas stocking he planned to send home to his children for Christmas. He shared that he stitches a piece each year that takes him many months to complete. Another individual uses crochet to make teddy bears and other stuffed animals to send home. Any of the above ideas will be time well spent when it comes to gifts for our children, when it comes to making a unique expression of the unending love we share for our children.

CARDS

Sending cards to my children is an exciting event. Sometimes the commissary had nice cards, but on special birthdays like number thirteen, I took poster board and made my own card. I took old magazines and cut out the letters, words, and photos I needed to complete my idea of how the card should look. Once I had my design thought out, I glued each piece or letter in place. The end result was always really cool and without a doubt it had "Dad's" personal touch. In my opinion, no card from the store could ever compare to those I hand made, and my children would agree. Also, I have sent handmade cards or letters congratulating them on a job well done, such as completing the school year with passing grades. You might consider making them some type of an award for this or any of their other accomplishments.

MAGAZINES

As mentioned previously, I was able to order magazine subscriptions for my children with the help of family and friends. I focused on magazines for which my children have strong interests. I asked them if they have a favorite magazine, or if given the chance, what magazine they would love to receive. You may also consider the idea of collecting various magazines so you can later use cutouts to make a collage to send to your children.

CUTOUTS

I enjoy reading a lot of magazines and often come across segments of a story that might appeal to my children's interests. For example, it might be a review on their favorite video game or on their favorite singer. Once they have received it, the article provides us with another opportunity for a future discussion and discovery.

SHARING BOOKS

I thoroughly enjoy reading a good book. One way that I have taken an interest in my children and have been able to bond is through sharing a book. At my former institution, they had a book fair usually twice a year in which you could purchase books categorized by age group and gender for your children. After purchase, the books are sent to your children from you. They sold other knickknacks such as bookmarks and erasers. If your institution does not offer these or your financial resources are limited, I suggest you seek age appropriate books from your family, friends, or volunteer organizations.

Another way I have shared books with my children is by asking them what book they really enjoyed reading. I purchase the book for myself and read it. We'd later discuss the favorite scenes, characters, and other aspects of the book. I have also ordered my children books from independent book sellers, as well as by family members or friends ordering online at vendors such as Amazon. I once read that a person who reads lives a thousand lives and a person who does not lives only one.

VIDEO STORYTIME

During my incarceration, I've been fortunate to participate, at least three times, in a story time program for my children. You had to meet certain criteria in order to participate. However, the only cost to the parent was the postage involved to send the book and recorded DVD. I picked out a free age appropriate book and read the beginning chapter to my children while being recorded on video. During the recording, I was allowed to take a moment to express a few other sentiments. I used this opportunity to send a loving message, a book, and a DVD of "dad" to my children. I encourage you to participate if ever given the opportunity to do so.

SCHOOL WORK

I often ask my children what they are currently learning at school. I try to ask specifics. I remember once sending my son a sample essay in order to help him if needed. On another occasion, I took a basic math class to freshen up my math skills in case my children needed any help with their work. I inquire regularly about their grades, and how well they are doing in school. More often than not, I get less than accurate responses, but they know I am concerned, nonetheless. To get more accurate updates as it relates to school and grades, I check with their mother or ask for a copy of their latest report card.

MOVIES

I have viewed some really great movies over the years. Some were funny, some scary, and others presented a great message about family values and relationships. I ask my children if they have viewed these movies so we can discuss them. On occasion, when I see one that presents a strong heartfelt message and one of inspiration, I send the DVD directly to them via whatever outlet is available to me at the time. Thanks to a family friend and his willingness to help, I'm able to contribute in this way. The movies I choose to send deal with life's challenges and how to overcome them. I feel it's one small way that I can encourage my children to grow and develop their own values, not only by viewing them on their own, but through our later discussions about them.

MUSIC

I really enjoy listening to music. I think most people can agree that music is connected to a person's soul. Music resonates with me in so many different ways and always stirs some type of emotion in me. My taste in music varies greatly. I enjoy conversations with my children about their favorite songs or artists. I watched their choice in music swing from one end to the other over the years. It makes me smile and gives my heart a sense of joy. I know that they are growing and becoming independent. They are discovering who they are and what they like in their choice of music.

At times, I would listen to a song and all the words seemed perfect as to what I wanted to relay to my children. During those times, I dedicated the song to my children. In my letters, I wrote down the lyrics so they could read along while they listened to the song. On other occasions, I have picked out various songs or made a playlist. I usually write a few notes out by the song. For example, "Your mom and me used to jam out to this one. Believe it or not, your mom loved this song." This shows my children that even though as parents our taste in music may have changed a bit, we are still like them.

My son sometimes likes to share recent news about a particular artist or what may be happening in his or her life, good or bad, which allows us an opportunity to look at what they could have done differently. On these occasions, as a father, I have the opportunity to discuss the consequences of the choices a person they care about makes. In other words, this becomes a teaching moment between parent and child. In addition, I enjoy listening to sample music clips on our institution music service, so I can share with my son which songs I enjoy. As you can see, when it comes to music, there are countless ways for us as parents to relate, connect, and bond with our children.

RELIGIOUS STUDY

Whatever your culture or religious beliefs may be, you can also share this with your children. Make sure its age appropriate material. Over the years I have been enrolled in a number of various outside free Bible correspondence courses. Many of these will enroll the children of incarcerated parents for free as well. My children were never interested in enrolling but have allowed me to discuss my beliefs and to pray with them regularly. One son asked me questions about baptism. I was grateful that my son was not only taking this step, but he included me in his decision. I encourage you not to preach to your children but rather share with them by example your faith and its principles.

Afterward

When this book idea crossed my mind, I seriously doubted the possibility of it becoming a reality. However, with a dear friend's encouragement, inspiration, and continued support, we sat down to discuss the possibilities of just that, making it become a reality.

I've heard the recommendation more than once that when it comes to writing a book, the writer is encouraged to write what they know. No one can question the fact that I'm a father. Well, I guess they could, but it would be pointless. I can certainly attest to the fact that I am the father of my wonderful sons, yet on the other hand, my abilities to be a successful one while incarcerated could be debated.

Wouldn't it be wonderful if we as men and women were all born as the perfect parents, that we knew all the right ways and right things to do and say without any learning necessary? Unfortunately, none of us are born with this prior knowledge. Much of what we learn about being a parent is learned or passed on to us by our own parents, and in turn, their behaviors were passed on to them by their parents, and so forth. The fact that parents are human beings tells me that none of us are perfect. Some may think so, and indeed do a better job at parenting than others, however, that doesn't mean the rest of us cannot make improvements in our lives along the way at being the best parents we can be. Change in us requires our commitment, effort, and time, but the most important realization to make is that change in us is necessary. If it weren't for change, we couldn't transform ourselves into the attentive and loving parents our children need.

My initial idea for this book was to make it a step by step guide for parents who were incarcerated and who wanted to improve their relationships with their children. Once I put my pen to paper and began to write, the book became so much more than just a guide. It became real. It became powerful. It became a testament of my efforts to stay connected with my children while incarcerated. Sharing my family history and other personal aspects of my life was not easy to do. The whole process was both frightening and vulnerable, yet therapeutic for me in the end.

I once read words from Chief Seattle's letter written in 1852, in response to the government inquiry to buy tribal lands. I don't think there are any better words that are more appropriate and related to personal growth, community outreach, and parenthood than these. He wrote:

"Until we know our fear, we cannot know our hope, until we know our suffering, we cannot know our joy. Until we know our turmoil, we cannot know our peace. Until we parent ourselves, we cannot parent our children. We cannot heal others until we understand healing. We cannot love others until we experience love. We cannot teach others until we have become conscious. We cannot teach justice until we understand balance."

All these thoughts resonate with me now, and although I have more lessons to learn, I have lived through a complete transformation from my former self.

I make no excuses for my dad's parenting styles or lack of them. Moreover, I make no excuses for mine. Although my dad fell short in being the dad that "I wanted him to be," he was the only dad he knew how to be. I see that now. My dad did the best that he could with what he was given. Although his capacity to love may have been limited, he loved me the only way that he knew how. Throughout my childhood, my dad was a very hard worker and provider. He wanted nothing more than for me to be happy and safe. As a kind and generous man, he was willing to go out of his way for most everyone. He was loved and is missed by many, especially me. If he was with me right now, I would say to him, "Dad, please forgive me. I am sorry for not being the best son that I could be to you. What do you need from me as your son? I want our relationship to improve and for us to become closer. I love you, Dad." At this stage in my awareness, I don't know what more I could say to make things right with him.

I've mentioned self-reflection and self-examination many times throughout this book. There is one thing certain about prison. Prisoners are given, seemingly, an endless amount of time to think and contemplate past decisions. I've had years, thousands of days, and tens of thousands of hours to think about my past actions. I have recalled literally hundreds of events when my behavior was inappropriate and destructive to another. The pain that I have caused at times to others and myself has been immense in my estimation. I have been fortunate that some of the people I've hurt and have made amends to accept my apologies and have forgiven me. However, others who I love dearly are not ready to forgive. Because of this, my heart remains heavy, yet my burden is lightened each day because of my faith in love and compassion. I want to take this moment to express to every person that I have hurt that I am truly sorry for the pain I caused you. I had no right to hurt you. May you be restored. May you be happy and healthy and whole once again. If I could go back and do things differently, I certainly would do so. Each of you deserves joy, peace, and freedom from any chains of suffering that may bind you. Again, I am sincerely sorry for all my wrongs and pray you will one day find forgiveness in your heart.

I offer with a sincere heart my prayer for you parents who are currently incarcerated. May you have the courage needed to commit to change, the strength to persevere, and the tenacity to heal. May you discover who you are and where you want to go. May you re-establish long-lost relationships with your children and repair others. May you make a connection with a power greater than yourselves. May you find joy, peace, and freedom. May you always share yourselves and openly express your love to your children.

I offer the following prayers for the children of those incarcerated. May they have an open and forgiving heart. May they see their parents for more than their past failures. May they be willing to share their lives and feelings with their parents. May their love for their parents bridge every separation.

I once read the old saying that time heals everything. I do not believe this to be an absolute, however time is constant and in time our thoughts, feelings, and emotions can change. It's been just over a year since my release and I'm grateful to say that much has improved for the better in my relationship with my sons. Since my release, resentment has turned to forgiveness, and our bond has only strengthened. Fortunately, I get to see my children often. We exercise, laugh and love together. I've had the privilege of helping one learn to drive and teaching the other the valuable importance of practicing a healthy lifestyle. Each day brings us closer and allows for new opportunities of sharing our lives together while making new memories.

I encourage you to never give upon your hopes and dreams of one day being re-united with your child/children. In the meantime, take advantage and seize this moment by being the best parent you can be to your child/children.

If sharing my life helps inspire or encourage one parent or one child to reach out to the other, it will have been all worth it. Remember, it's never too late to say, "I love you."

Sincerely,

William J. Patterson

William J. Patterson

Special Note to the Incarcerated

My goal with this book is to change lives, even if it's just one incarcerated parent at a time. I enjoy hearing from inmates and would like to hear from those who have read my book, especially if you were inspired or helped by the book. All feedback is welcomed and much appreciated. I may not be able to correspond to each and every email, but I will definitely be thinking of you and your children. I'll pray for both you and your family. I pray your love for your children will bridge every separation.

God Bless You,

William

William

Contact William J. Patterson at:

williamjpattersonbooks@gmail.com

Parent to Parent

Appendix

6-13-16

I have questions for you. Call it a little homework assignment. Please take your time and answer truthfully in your own words. Be honest and don't worry about my feelings. I'm asking these because I want to be the best possible dad I can be for you. Thank you for your answers. I look forward to reading them and working on any changes. I love and miss you. Feel free to add anything else you might think of ok. Love Always,

Dad

① How Can I be a better dad? You already are There is No one that could ever take Your plac

② What do I need to stop doing? nothing

③ If I could change one thing about me as a dad what would it be? Think positivly

④ What are one or two things you need most from me as a dad? The Love and support that you have always givin me

78

6·18·16

I have some questions for you, a little homework I guess you can say. It's because I want to be the absolute best dad I can be for you. Please take your time, answer in your own way and mail back to me, in the envelope. Thank you. I love and miss you more than words can express

① How can I be a better dad? Theres way To be a Betkr Tan great

② What do I need to stop doing? I Dont no you do anything wrong

③ If I could change one thing about me as a dad what would it be? nothing.

④ What are one or two things you need most from me as a dad? I ypont no you already gave my love and jo mich.

*A poem written for **** 06-10-2018*

Locked Away

Every day while locked away,
There's so much I want to say.
Phone calls are so very short,
There's often very little new to report.
The days here can be long,
With constant thoughts of going home.
Day becomes night, night becomes day,
Why does it have to be this way?
Writing letters helps me think,
Words from my heart never go blank.
They come with remorse, regret and shame,
After all, I have no one but me to blame.
I caused this storm in my life,
Full of hurt, heartache and strife.
It's up to me now to become a new man,
Making changes and creating a plan.
I do what I can from here,
Until we can all be near.
What a day that will be, just you wait and see.
The new dad I've become, once I am free.

A poem written for **** 05-22-2018

My Name Is ****

Hello, my name is ****.
I said ****, Not Brian.
Get it right man, show some respect, not neglect.
This world can be cruel, but I prefer to be cool.
Love works best unlike the rest,
Compassion, kindness and faith rule,
Shining out from me like a jewel.
I wear my armor well,
Armed like a knight fighting in Hell.
God is my General, I am his soldier,
Just imagine me when I become older.
Life is a series of events always changing with time,
One after another all waiting in line.
They fall like dominos, but I am ready,
Because my Lord is King, my mind is steady.
I stand strong like the oldest trees in the forest,
Roots of wisdom, branches of steel, and leaves that can kill.
The sun will set, the sun will rise,
I will continue to improvise.
Raindrops will come, raindrops will go,
But in the end there's always a rainbow.
As God smiles down on me, He will always see,
That I'm no quitter, but the team's best hitter.
His promise to me is that I will be,
In his loving arms, you'll one day see.

CHILD DEVELOPMENT, PARENTING STRATEGIES, AND CAUSE FOR CONCERN

Age	Child		Parent	
	Developmentally appropriate behavior	Causes for concern	Parenting strategies	Causes for concern
0–3 months	• Reacts and turns toward sound • Watches faces and follows objects • Coos and babbles • Becomes more expressive and develops a social smile • Develops a general routine of sleep/wake times	• Is unable to move each limb separately from the others • Has difficulty tracking light or faces • Regularly cries for hours at a time and is very hard to calm	• Don't be afraid of "spoiling" your baby; hold, cuddle, and comfort him often • Respond to your baby's cries and provide the comfort he needs (rocking, feeding, diaper changing) • Give the baby lots of attention (talk, sing, read, play), and read the cues to recognize when he needs a break • Have conversations with your baby acting as if you understand each other • Allow the baby to explore through movement, taste, and touch, but set safe limits • Provide time on the floor for sitting, rolling, and crawling	• Does not know when to feed or tries to keep the baby on a rigid schedule • Feels too much attention or holding will spoil the baby • Has trouble knowing when the baby is hungry, needs attention, or needs quiet time • Gets upset every time the baby cries • Allows the baby to cry for a long time without trying to comfort • Doesn't enjoy time with the baby or feel the baby's personality "fits in" with family
4–7 months	• Babbles chains of sounds • Responds to others' expressions of emotions • Grasps and holds objects • Regards own hand and explores objects with hand and mouth • Sits with, and then without, support on hands	• Cannot hold head up or roll over • Does not make sounds in response to attention • Consistently resists all efforts to hold or comfort • Shows little interest in exploration • Strongly resists a routine of sleep and awake time		

Child Development, Parenting Strategies, and Causes for Concern, 0–18 years (Continued)

Age	Child		Parent	
	Developmentally appropriate behavior	Causes for concern	Parenting strategies	Causes for concern
8–12 months	• Changes tone when babbling • Says "dada" and "mama" and uses exclamations • Imitates sounds and gestures • Explores in many ways (shaking, dropping, banging, poking) • Pulls self up to stand and may walk briefly without help	• Is not able to calm himself sometimes • Does not babble or make simple gestures • Fails to respond to name or simple verbal requests • Does not crawl or explore the area • Has little or no reaction when parent(s) leave the room or return	*Continued from previous page*	*Continued from previous page*
2 years	• Says several single words and two- or three-word phrases • Follows simple instructions • Points to things when named • Finds hidden objects • Scribbles • Stands alone and walks well	• Knows no single words • Does not walk easily • Does not seem to know or respond to family members • Does not amuse himself for short periods of time	• Offer a variety of sensory experiences and follow the toddler's lead in play • Encourage, but don't rush, motor development—provide plenty of safe, low places to walk and climb • Create predictable routines and rituals	• Is cold and unresponsive toward the child • Rarely praises the child or shows affection • Has trouble dealing with own or the child's anger • Focuses more on the child's negative behaviors

This material may be freely reproduced and distributed. However, when doing so, please credit Child Welfare Information Gateway. Available online at http://www.childwelfare.gov/pubs/braindevtrauma.cfm

Child Development, Parenting Strategies, and Causes for Concern, 0–18 years (Continued)

	Child		Parent	
Age	Developmentally appropriate behavior	Causes for concern	Parenting strategies	Causes for concern
3 years	• Uses four- to five-word sentences • Follows two- or three-part instructions • Recognizes and identifies most common objects • Draws simple straight or circular lines • Climbs well, walks up and down stairs, runs	• No two-word spontaneous phrases • Has trouble expressing emotions • Often refuses to do simple tasks • Seems overly fearful, even in safe situations	*Continued from previous page* • Be a safe, reliable base as the child explores the world around him • Tell stories and talk with the child about what they see, hear, and do • Listen and try to understand what the child is saying • Take the child's emotions seriously and help him make sense of them • Support interaction with peers; provide structure but otherwise let him negotiate playtime on his own	*Continued from previous page* • Frequently yells at the child or punishes accidents harshly • Describes the child as having hostile intentions, i.e., "He doesn't like me" or "He knows better" • Pushes the child too hard to do too many activities and/or finds it hard to let the child try things by himself • Has trouble setting consistent rules and safe limits
4 years	• Uses five- to six-word sentences, tells stories • Understands counting and may know some numbers • Identifies four or more colors • Copies or draws simple shapes • Walks/runs forward and backward with balance	• Is unable to run, jump, or climb easily • Is extremely aggressive and hostile toward peers • Clings and gets very upset when parent leaves		

This material may be freely reproduced and distributed. However, when doing so, please credit Child Welfare Information Gateway. Available online at http://www.childwelfare.gov/pubs/braindevtrauma.cfm

Child Development, Parenting Strategies, and Causes for Concern, 0–18 years (Continued)

Age	Child		Parent	
	Developmentally appropriate behavior	Causes for concern	Parenting strategies	Causes for concern
5 years	• Speaks in full sentences, tells longer stories • Draws circles and squares, begins to copy letters • Climbs, hops, swings, and may skip • Tries to solve problems from a single point of view and identify solutions to conflicts • More likely to agree to rules	• Does not speak full sentences or speak clearly enough for strangers to understand • Seems shy and very fearful with other children • Never shares or takes turns • Regularly has difficulty caring for own toilet needs	• Help child take on new responsibilities • Teach reasonable risks and safe limits • Handle anger constructively • Create a safe environment where your child can feel comfortable talking about a wide range of issues and emotions • Share feelings and stories about how to deal with problems and face fears • Support healthy friendships and encourage appropriate social activities	• Regularly finds the child's behavior unmanageable • Does not see the need for the child to socialize with others • Thinks the child is too aggressive or too dependent • Often criticizes or blames the child • Seems excessively anxious about the responsibilities of being a parent • Leaves the child alone for extended periods of time • Is not involved with school or with other parents of children the same age
6–7 years	• Reads short words and sentences • Draws person or animal • Takes pride and pleasure in mastering new skills • Has more internal control over emotions and behaviors • Shows growing awareness of good and bad	• Is frequently sad, worried, afraid, or withdrawn • Is easily hurt by peers • Bullies other children • Develops unrealistic fears (phobias)		

This material may be freely reproduced and distributed. However, when doing so, please credit Child Welfare Information Gateway. Available online at http://www.childwelfare.gov/pubs/braindevtrauma.cfm

Child Development, Parenting Strategies, and Causes for Concern, 0–18 years (Continued)

	Child		Parent	
Age	Developmentally appropriate behavior	Causes for concern	Parenting strategies	Causes for concern
8–10 years	• Reads well • Multiplies numbers • Expresses a unique personality when relating to others • Solves conflicts by talking, not fighting • Is able to "bounce back" from most disappointments	• Returns to baby-like or silly behaviors • Is preoccupied with violent movies, TV, video games • Is fearful with familiar adults, or too friendly with strangers	*Continued from previous page*	*Continued from previous page*
11–14 years	• May have frequent mood swings or changes in feelings • Gradually develops own taste, sense of style, and identity • Has a hobby, sport, or activity • Learns to accept disappointments and overcome failures • Has one or more "best" friends and positive relationships with others the same age	• Eats or sleeps less (or more) than before • Has strong negative thoughts or opinions of himself • Has an extreme need for approval and social support • Has highly conflicted relationships or regularly causes family conflicts • Is alone most of the time and seems happier alone than with others	• Establish fair and consistent rules • Provide opportunities for new, challenging experiences • Address the potential consequences of risky behaviors • Help teens resolve conflicts, solve problems, and understand changing emotions • Encourage goals for the future and help create systems for time and task management • Discuss the physical changes in puberty that affect height, weight, and body shape	• Worries that the child is maturing very early or very late • Doesn't set reasonable limits for the child's behavior • Is uninterested in helping the child address overwhelming emotions or situations • Expects the child to adhere to strict rules and severely punishes mistakes • Often has conflicts and loses temper with the child • Frequently criticizes, nags, or judges the child

This material may be freely reproduced and distributed. However, when doing so, please credit Child Welfare Information Gateway. Available online at http://www.childwelfare.gov/pubs/braindevtrauma.cfm

Child Development, Parenting Strategies, and Causes for Concern, 0–18 years (Continued)

	Child		Parent	
Age	Developmentally appropriate behavior	Causes for concern	Parenting strategies	Causes for concern
15–18 years	• Begins to develop an identity and self-worth beyond body image and physical appearance • Is able to calm down and handle anger • Sets goals and works toward achieving them • Accepts family rules, completes chores and other responsibilities • Needs time for emotions and reasoning skills to catch up with rapid physical changes	• Feels hopeless, unable to make things better • Withdraws from family or friends • Often gives in to negative peer pressure • Becomes violent or abusive • Drives aggressively, speeds, drinks and drives • Has a favorable attitude toward drug use • Diets excessively, even when not overweight	*Continued from previous page* • Be available for help and advice when needed • Tolerate (within reason) teen's developing likes and dislikes in clothes, hairstyles, and music	*Continued from previous page* • Doesn't provide the child any privacy and finds it overly difficult to "let go" as he becomes more independent

RECOMMENDED READING

Alone in the World: Children of Incarcerated (2005) Nell Berristein

Celebrate Recovery Inside (1986) John Baker & Rick Warren

Forgiveness: How to Make Peace with Your Past and Get On with Your Life (1991) Dr. Sidney B. & Suzanne Simon

How to be a Responsible Father: A Workbook for Offenders (2007) Terry L. Stawar, Ed.D.

Inside Out Dad: Fathering Handbook (2005) National Fatherhood Initiative

Life Beyond Loss: A workbook for Incarcerated Men (1999) Beverly Welo

Making Peace with Your Past (2001) Harold Bloomfield M.D.

Parenting from Prison: A Hands On Guide For Incarcerated Parents (2011) James Birney

Parenting From the Inside Out (2000) Dan Siegel

Planet Middle School Dr. Kevin Leman

Raising Cain: Protecting the Emotional Life of Boys (2000) Dan Kindlon & Michael Thompson

Real Boys: Rescuing Our Sons from the Myth of Boyhood (1999) William Pollack Ph.D.

Real Boys: Voices (2000) William Pollack Ph.D.

The Available Parent (2011) Dr. John Duffy

The Heart of Parenting: How to Raise an Emotionally Intelligent Child (1997) John Gottman

Toxic Parents: Overcoming Their Hurtful Legacy & Reclaiming Your Life (1989) Susan Forward Ph.D.

Uncommon Manhood: Secrets to What It Means To Be a Man (2012) Tony Dungy

BOOKS FOR CHILDREN OF INCARCERATED PARENTS

Bender, Janet. *My Daddy is in Jail* (2003) Chapin, South Carolina 29036: YouthLight (5-11-year olds).

Brisson, Pat. *Mama Loves Me from Away*, (2004) illustrated by Laurie Caple. Boyds Mills Press, 815 Church Street, Honesdale, Pennsylvania 18431 (5-10-year olds).

Butterworth, Oliver. *A Visit to the Big House* (1993) Boston, Massachusetts: Houghton Mifflin Company (7-10-year olds).

Center for Children with Incarcerated Parents. *I Know How You Feel Because This Happened to Me* (1984) Berkeley, California 94708: Prison MATCH (7-8-year olds).

Channing Bete Company. *Sara Visits her Dad in Prison* (2004) South Deerfield, Maine, (young children who will visit).

Gaffney, Linda. *My Daddy Does Good Things, Too! A Book for (and about) Children of Incarcerated Parents* (2006) Olympia, Washington: Homeplace Press.

Hickman, Martha W. and Larry Raymond. *When Andy's Father Went to Prison* (1990) Morton Grove, Illinois: Albert Whitman & Company.

Maury, Inez. *My Mother and I Are Growing Stronger/ Mi Mama Y Yo nos Hacemos Fuertes* (1979) New Seed Press, PO Box 9488, Berkeley, California. Spanish/English book (5-12-year olds).

St. Pierre, Stephanie. *Everything You Need to Know When a Parent Is in Jail* (1994) Rosen Publishing Group, New York, New York.

Whitmore Hickman, Martha. *When Andy's Father Went to Prison* (1990) Albert Whitman and Company, 5747 Howard Street, Niles, Illinois (5-11 years olds).

Wittbold, Maureen. *Let's Talk about When your Parent is in Jail* (2002) New York: Rosen Publishing Group (5-12-year olds).

SUPPORT GROUP INFORMATION FOR
INCARCERATED PARENTS

(If possible, readers should check out websites first to make sure contact and services offered are up to date.)

Cabrini Green Legal Aid (IL only)
6 South Clark St., Suite 200, Chicago, IL 60603
(312) 738-2452, ext. 6
cgla.net

Services: Advice and some legal representation for incarcerated parents and family in IL on guardianship (short-term or court-ordered), visitation, and child custody, plus advice on foster care and divorce cases. They can also send a free Illinois-focused resource guide; *Caring for Children When a Parent is Arrested*.

Family Financial Corrections Network (website only)
fcnetwork.org

Services: Primarily provides online resources for families of prisoners related to parenting, children of prisoners, prison visitation, mothers and fathers in prison, etc. This organization does not mail out information. All materials must be downloaded from the web.

Fatherhood.gov
(877) 432-3411
help@fatherhood.gov/info

Friends Outside
P.O. Box 4085, Stockton, CA 95204
(209) 955-0701

They provide services to prisoners and their families. They also provide pre-release and parenting programs at all California State Prisons (through case management). They operate visitor's centers at all California State Prisons, too. Write for a free publication – *Children of Incarcerated Parents, The Bill of Rights,* and *How to Tell Children about Jail and Prisons.*

Legal Services for Prisoners with Children
4400 Market St., Oakland, CA 94608
(415) 255-7036
prisonerswithchildren.org

Services: Answers letters, mostly about family law; sends self-help legal manuals (in Spanish and English) on your question, and helps you find info. Their expertise is mostly in CA; they're less able to answer questions from other states. Letters should be as specific as possible. No direct representation.

National Fatherhood Initiative
12410 Milestone Center Drive, Suite 600, Germantown, MD 20876
(301) 948-0599
Email: info@fatherhood.org
fatherhood.org

Services: Provides (for a fee) the resources to establish a re-entry program for incarcerated fathers called Inside out Dad. Its website includes a large number of free resources.

National Resource Center on Children and Families of the Incarcerated
NRC-CFI at Rutgers-Camden, 405-7 Cooper St. Room 103, Camden, NJ 08102
(865) 225-2718
nrccfi@camden.rutgers.edu
nrccfi.camden.rutgers.edu

Services: Primarily provides research, fact sheets, and a program directory related to families of prisoners, parenting, children of prisoners, prison visitation, mothers and fathers in prison, etc.

National Responsible Fatherhood Clearing House
2394 Mt. Vernon Rd, Suite 210
Dunwoody, GA 30338

Prison Fellowship
44180 Riverside Pkwy, Lansdowne, VA 20176
Prisonfellowship.org
Email: info@pfm.org

Angel Tree Inquiries may call (800) 552-6435. Through Angel
Tree, a program of prison fellowship, your children can receive
gifts at Christmas with love from you. To share the love of Jesus
Christ, church volunteers buy gifts and give them to your
children with age-appropriate presentation of the gospel.
Contact your prison's chaplain to request a participation form or
write to them directly.

San Francisco Children of Incarcerated Parents Partnership
1569 Solano Ave #293
Berkeley, CA 94707
Email: sfcipp.info@gmail.com
www.sfcipp.org

2.4 million U.S. children have a parent behind bars today. The
partnership formed to improve the lives of incarcerated children
and to demand a "Bill of Rights" for them, downloadable from the
website in English and Spanish.

The Annie E. Casey Foundation
(410) 547-6600
701 St. Paul St.
Baltimore, MD 21202
aecf.org/resources/

U.S. Department of Health and Human Services Fatherhood
Initiative
330 C Street S.W.
Washington D.C. 20201
acf.hhs.gov/ofa/programs/healthy-marriage/responsible-
fatherhood

Prison Activist Resource Center

PO Box 70447

Oakland, CA 94612

People incarcerated may write for a free 24-page resource directory.

CreativeChild.com

A national monthly publication and website that provides parents with the latest information on how to nurture their child's creativity.

Save Kids of Incarcerated Parents

Skipinc.org

669 Bush Drive

Hope Hull, AL 36043

or

PO Box 25347

Montgomery, AL 36125

(334)549-9674   info@skipinc.org

Founded in Florida with chapters in Georgia, Michigan and Texas. Provides support services to children of incarcerated parents and their families through education, advocacy and research.

Children of Incarcerated Parents Youth.gov

US Government website that helps maintain and strengthen effective youth programs. Included are youth facts, funding information and tools to help you assess community assets, generate maps of local and federal resources, search for evidence-based youth programs, and keep up to date on the latest, youth-related news.

Rainbow.org

Rainbow Headquarters

614 Dempster St

William J. Patterson

Suite C
Evanston, IL 60202
847-952-1770

Rainbows programs help children who are grieving the loss of a parent or guardian due to death, divorce, deployment and trauma. Rainbows trained facilitators, using age-appropriate curriculum, establish peer support groups in schools, faith-based organization, or community centers. Also, programs for children of incarcerated parents.

National Mentoring Resource Center.org

Incarcerated Mothers Advocacy Project (IMAP)

IMAP is a coalition of law students, attorneys, social service providers and formerly incarcerated women who seek to change the rights afforded to incarcerated and previously incarcerated women in Washington. To get involved with IMAP contact Erika Pablo-Koche at koche1410@gmail.com

Centerhealthyminds.org
Supporting kids of incarcerated parents.
625 W Washington Ave.
Madison, WI 53703

Have your family member or other search Google or other search engines for local support groups in your particular city, state or region.

About the Author

William J. Patterson is author of *Chapter 7 Bankruptcy: Seven Steps to Financial Freedom*. He is a lifetime resident of Tennessee. He enjoys the great outdoors and exploring new adventures with his sons, family members, and friends.

In his second book: *Parent to Parent – Raising Children from Prison*, Mr. Patterson shares his most intimate and personal life experiences as an incarcerated parent in order to encourage and inspire other parents to stay connected with their children.

Besides exploring his newest book ideas, he is invested with several advocacy groups that assist inmates and families in their efforts toward a successful return to society for the benefit of all.

Summary

Parent to Parent – Raising Children from Prison entails the raw, painful, and real emotions a parent experiences while incarcerated and separated from their children. It explains how a parent must discover, understand, and explore themselves before they can be beneficial to their children. The book centers on my story and how I used many resources including, but not limited to, self-reflection and self-examination in order to overcome the many past hurts I experienced. I discuss the importance of achieve and maintaining mental and physical health, and in other chapters the difference between discipline and punishment, the importance of communication, healing, forgiveness, and love. Also, I offer more in-depth discussions as well as techniques and ideas of how parents can be actively involved with their children while incarcerated. Once a parent begins to make changes in their own life, then they can begin to be a positive influence on their children's lives.

In the appendix I have provided examples of some of my own correspondence between my children and me, carts of child development, parenting strategies, and cause for concern, a recommended reading list for both parents and children, and support group information for incarcerated parents.

Chapter 7 Bankruptcy:
Seven Steps to Financial Freedom

CHAPTER 7 BANKRUPTCY
Seven Steps to Financial Freedom

William J. Patterson

Only $22.99

plus $7 S/H with tracking

SOFTCOVER, 8" x 10", 240+ pages

Much of bankruptcy procedure is technical and very straight forward. More often than not, there is only one way to complete a required form and only one set of rules that apply to that form. Being familiar with the legal system, prisoners understand that one misstep can cost you your freedom. With Chapter 7 Bankruptcy, your financial freedom is at stake.

This book is designed to be an all-inclusive resource guide with step-by-step instructions for prisoners filing their own Chapter 7. It details the basic information on different aspects of federal bankruptcy laws, as well as the author's own personal experience in filing a successful Chapter 7 claim.

Here are sample forms, schedules, and instructions you need to obtain your financial freedom! In these pages you will learn a wealth of information and have the technical points explained in easy to follow language. Also featured is a basic explanation of the different chapters under which a bankruptcy case may be filed and answers to some of the most commonly asked questions about the bankruptcy process.

The goal of this work is to help you through all of the steps, to point out obstacles along the way and resources both inside and outside of prison, and finally, to provide you with inspiration and encouragement that you too can do this on your own. With preparation, patience, and perseverance, you can accomplish anything – including the successful discharge of your own Chapter 7 Bankruptcy. If you follow these 7 basic steps to completing a Chapter 7 Bankruptcy, you too can enjoy the freedoms that a fresh start will provide.

The Best 500+

WE NEED YOUR
REVIEWS

Rate Us & Win!

We do monthly drawings for a FREE copy of one of our publications. Just have your loved one rate any Freebird Publishers book on Amazon and then send us a quick e-mail with your name, inmate number, and institution address and you could win a FREE book.

FREEBIRD PUBLISHERS
Box 541
North Dighton, MA 02764

www.freebirdpublishers.com
Diane@FreebirdPublishers.com

Thanks for your interest in
Freebird Publishers!

We value our customers and would love to hear from you! Reviews are an important part in bringing you quality publications. We love hearing from our readers-rather it's good or bad (though we strive for the best)!

If you could take the time to review/rate any publication you've purchased with Freebird Publishers we would appreciate it!

If your loved one uses Amazon, have them post your review on the books you've read. This will help us tremendously, in providing future publications that are even more useful to our readers and growing our business.

Amazon works off of a 5 star rating system. When having your loved one rate us be sure to give them your chosen star number as well as a written review. Though written reviews aren't required, we truly appreciate hearing from you.

☆☆☆☆☆ **Everything a prisoner needs is available in this book.**
January 30, 201 June 7, 2018
Format: Paperback

A necessary reference book for anyone in prison today. This book has everything an inmate needs to keep in touch with the outside world on their own from inside their prison cell. Inmate Shopper's business directory provides complete contact information on hundreds of resources for inmate services and rates the companies listed too! The book has even more to offer, contains numerous sections that have everything from educational, criminal justice, reentry, LGBT, entertainment, sports schedules and more. The best thing is each issue has all new content and updates to keep the inmate informed on todays changes. We recommend everybody that knows anyone in prison to send them a copy, they will thank you.

* No purchase neccessary. Reviews are not required for drawing entry. Void where prohibited.
Contest date runs July 1 - June 30, 2019.

   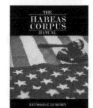

  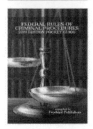 

  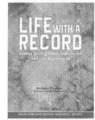 

S.T.O.P : Start Thinking Outside Prison
Inspiring Motivating Self-Help

Regain Your Power Beyond Prison Walls

Greatness lies within many of my brothers and sisters. The problem is we tend to find ourselves incarcerated before we discover this greatness. Our thought patterns and consistent inability to think on a positive level leads us straight to prison.

Thinking is very critical to one's success, failure, and survival. Every decision requires thinking. If not, many actions will be done on impulse. And impulsive behavior tends to bring about situations from which one needs to be rescued. Think of a preteen, teenager, or young adult, all of whom can possess the impulsive behaviors of children. If the impulses aren't tamed or controlled, the behavior patterns will be present in each stage of life. Maybe this is the reason I see so many 40-year-olds that lack self-control or the ability to deal with some of life's simplest problems. They can't attack the situations from a professional, calm, and diplomatic standpoint.

S.T.O.P. was written as a movement to help promote a greater thinking process - a thinking process I believe will slow down the recidivism rate within our communities. This will mean that more fathers will be available in the household, more parents around to pass down the guidance that will enable our young boys to become men. Men who will stand accountable for the direction of their community.

As a man, I ask all men to join together and help rebuild what many of us helped destroy. It starts with you. It starts with me. No outside force can aid this cause until the aid is given from within. A better future is literally in our hands. It is my intent that the following ten chapters will provide enlightenment and force all of us to S.T.O.P. - Start Thinking Outside Prison!

Softcover, 6" x 9", 70+ Pgs., B&W Interior

Ask. Believe. Receive.
Our Power to Create Our Own Destiny

In life, true strength comes from never letting an experience define you. There is always a reason for everything – steppingstones on a path to better destinations.

Our words have immense creative power and determine where our paths will lead us. If we put positive words into the world we create reality from with them.

"Positive, creative and powerful," is how the Bible says we were created, and it explains the capabilities we all possess from birth.

We are gods – creators. We create our destiny with our words ... good or bad ... and we are responsible. Of course, that means that we are always capable of changing the course of our lives, by speaking good words.

This book will literally change your life and hopefully open your eyes to your own creative power.

A must-read for everyone!

A man's future consists of the faith inside of him. Whatever that faith is, so shall it become his reality. – The Bhagavagita

Softcover, 6" x 9", 92 Pgs., B&W Interior

107

Made in United States
Orlando, FL
14 March 2023

31022837R00063